AQA Business Studies

GCSE

Peter Stimpson
Rachel Sumner
Thomas Ramsbottom
Andrew Hammond
Nigel Straker

Series editor
Tim Chapman

Published in 2009 by:
Nelson Thornes Ltd
Delta Place
27 Bath Road
CHELTENHAM
GL53 7TH
United Kingdom

12 13 / 10 9 8 7 6 5 4

A catalogue record for this book is available from the British Library

ISBN 978-1-4085-0435-2

Cover photograph: by Alamy/Nick Gregory
Illustrations by Angela Knowles; additional illustrations by eMC Design Ltd

Page make-up by eMC Design Ltd, www.emcdesign.org.uk

Printed in China by 1010 Printing International Ltd

Contents

Nelson Thornes has worked in partnership with AQA to make sure that this book offers you the best possible support for your GCSE course. All the content has been approved by the senior examining team at AQA, so you can be sure that it gives you just what you need when you are preparing for your exams.

■ How to use this book

This book covers everything you need for your course.

Learning Objectives

At the beginning of each section or topic you'll find a list of Learning Objectives based on the requirements of the specification, so you can make sure you are covering everything you need to know for the exam.

Objectives

Objectives

Objectives

Objectives

First objective.

Second objective.

AQA Examiner's Tips

Don't forget to look at the AQA Examiner's Tips throughout the book to help you with your study and prepare for your exam.

AQA Examiner's tip

Don't forget to look at the AQA Examiner's Tips throughout the book to help you with your study and prepare for your exam.

AQA Examination-style Questions

These offer opportunities to practise doing questions in the style that you can expect in your exam so that you can be fully prepared on the day.

AQA examination questions are reproduced by permission of the Assessment and Qualifications Alliance.

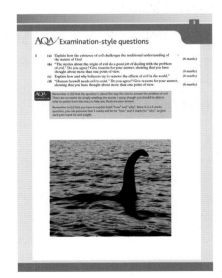

Visit **www.nelsonthornes.com/aqagcse** for more information.

AQA GCSE Business Studies

Business Studies is a subject that will give you the skills and knowledge to understand how businesses are set up and managed. Business activity is the basis of so much that we take for granted in our everyday lives.

Businesses provide us with:

- The goods that we buy in the shops and on the internet.
- The services such as leisure activities, holidays and mobile phone networks that we buy to make our lives more interesting and rewarding.
- Jobs that allow us to earn the wages and salaries that give us the means to choose what to buy.

Normal life in our country today would clearly not be possible without businesses!

To be able to do these very important things, businesses and the people who own and manage them have to:

- obtain important resources such as land, labour and machines
- research what people want to buy before using these resources to make goods and provide services
- produce these goods and services as efficiently as possible
- market the products to the right people, at the right prices and in a way that buyers will find convenient
- employ, train and motivate workers
- keep a record of all financial dealings so that the profit or loss of the business can be worked out.

Learning about all of these activities makes Business Studies one of the most exciting and relevant subjects, that you can study at GCSE. Throughout your course you will be encouraged to find out through your own research how some businesses are succeeding and some are failing – and what the key factors are that determine success or failure.

How will you be examined in GCSE Business Studies?

This will depend on the course that your school or college is entering you for.

AQA GCSE Business Studies

This has two written examination papers (Unit 1 and Unit 2) and one Controlled Assessment (Unit 3).

Unit 1 is a 1 hour paper, marked out of 60 and worth 40 per cent of the overall examination.

Unit 2 is a 1 hour paper, marked out of 60 and worth 35 per cent of the overall examination.

Unit 3 is the controlled assessment which is worth 25 per cent of the overall examination.

AQA GCSE Business Studies Short Course

This has one written examination paper (Unit 13) and one Controlled Assessment (Unit 14).

Unit 13 is a 1 hour paper, marked out of 40 and worth 50 per cent of the overall examination.

Unit 14 – very similar to Unit 3 above.

AQA GCSE Applied Business Double Award

This has four written examination papers (Unit 1 and a choice of two out of Units 4–6 plus Unit 7).

Unit 1 – the same as above.

The other units are NOT covered by this textbook.

So, if you are studying for any of these courses then this book will be invaluable to you for preparing for Units 1, 2 and 13.

What is this book about?

The purpose of this book is to provide you with all of the information, examples and question practice that you will need to do really well on the unit examinations mentioned above. It is split into TWO sections. These sections are as follows:

Unit 1   Setting up a business

This will prepare you for Units 1 (GCSE Business Studies) and 13 (GCSE Short Course).

It introduces you to the role of entrepreneurs – people who set up new businesses. It explains where new business ideas can come from. The section covers and explains all of the major decisions that new business owners have to take before setting up and serving their first customer!

Unit 2   Growing as a business

This will prepare you for Unit 2 (GCSE Business Studies).

It builds upon the ideas explained in Unit 1. This section considers the issues faced by larger and expanding businesses. Most new business owners hope that they will be successful enough to be able to manage a growing business. Marketing, finance, managing people and effective production techniques – these all feature in this easy-to-follow Unit.

In conclusion …

This book will be your guide and support during the one or two years of your Business Studies course. I hope you really enjoy your Business Studies experience and decide to study the subject at GCE and beyond. There is so much to learn about operating a successful business that Business Studies is now one of the most popular subject studied at university. Who knows, perhaps this book will set you on your way to a great career in business.

UNIT 1　Setting up a business

■ Introduction

In Unit 1 of GCSE Business Studies you will study many of the issues involved in starting up a business, operating it and the reasons for success or failure. These issues include:

- what it means to be an entrepreneur and where new business ideas 'come from'
- how a business is set up and the aims that are commonly set
- the legal structure of small businesses
- how owners of small businesses market their goods or services
- where finance comes from for setting up a business
- how to manage workers in a small firm
- why customer service is important and how products can be made.

You will also be introduced to four entrepreneurs who will appear throughout to illustrate some of the key points in Unit 1. The focus of this Unit is very much on the early stages of business start-up and therefore on small- to medium-sized businesses operating in national markets. You will also have the opportunity to explore real-life case studies based on newly created businesses operating in the UK today.

Unit 1 is divided into 5 chapters.

Chapter 1　Starting a business

You will study what it means to be an entrepreneur and understand the concept of 'enterprise'. You will begin to appreciate some of the risks and rewards associated with running your own business, and will look at some of the decisions that entrepreneurs need to make when setting up their business, such as the legal structure for their business, identifying its stakeholders and choosing where to locate the business. You will also begin to appreciate some of the tools that assist entrepreneurs in making these decisions – the setting of objectives and the development of a business plan.

Chapter 2   Marketing

This chapter will give you an introduction to marketing within a business with a limited budget to spend. You will discover that marketing is much more than just 'selling'. Research into the market will help to make the business successful – different approaches to marketing will be successful with different goods and services. One of the common themes in marketing decisions taken by many small businesses today is the importance of ICT.

Chapter 3   Finance

You will be introduced to the importance of finance to a new business. The chapter also looks at sources of finance and financial advice when setting up a small business.

You will soon become used to discussing financial terms such as 'cash flow forecast' and other key terms identified in this chapter.

Chapter 4   People in business

Every business needs someone to work in it! Sometimes the owner is enough but very often small businesses need to recruit workers. When people have been employed they need to be motivated to work well. The owners will also want to keep – or retain – the good workers and how they might do this is also explained.

Chapter 5   Operations management

Finally, you will be introduced to the importance of operational decisions in managing a successful small business – how goods can be made as efficiently as possible; how customers can be provided with good service and the increasing importance of ICT in informing and supporting customers.

■ Skills development

As well as learning about the ideas and theories related to Business Studies, you will also be encouraged to develop your skills during your GCSE course.

In Unit 1 we will be focussing on the development of two skill sets: research and enterprise.

Throughout the text you will see Research Activities with suggestions for skills-related tasks. They will encourage you to think about the development of each of these skills.

The Research Activities will be particularly beneficial in your preparation for the Controlled Assessment, Investigating small businesses (Unit 3).

Research activity

Identify an entrepreneur in your community and interview them to discover their business objectives for the current year.

■ Meet the entrepreneurs

Here are the four entrepreneurs who will appear in your text at various points to illustrate some of the key ideas and theories.

Nilesh

Decorates the homes of elderly and vulnerable members of the community.

Has worked in decorating for over 20 years.

Works alone.

Has an excellent reputation for good quality work.

Wants to help others.

Possesses excellent vocational skills, sound communication skills and attention to detail.

Ania

Began gardening when she was five years old, helping her grandfather on his allotment.

Has a degree in horticulture.

Set up her gardening business in 2005 using her own equipment in order to be her own boss.

Runs courses in growing vegetables this year for local school children.

Has very good work-related skills, is very organised and likes to plan ahead.

Alex

Develops websites from home.

Began business whilst studying ICT at sixth form college to earn money from hobby.

Has over two hundred customers across UK.

Wants to launch a website-hosting service next year.

Spends his leisure time writing computer games.

Alex is very creative and loves coming up with new ideas. He also has worked hard on developing his technical skills.

Minseung

Is currently studying for her GCSEs.

Earns money walking her neighbours dogs at the weekends and after school to help fund her studies.

Loves listening to music and hopes to study Performing Arts at college.

Minseung is caring and ambitious.

1 Starting a business

Introduction

In 2008 it was reported by *The Times* that small-business owners (entrepreneurs) are worth £1,046 billion to the UK economy, just in terms of the hours they work. In 2008, the Office of National Statistics (ONS) registered a 3 per cent increase in the number of businesses registered in the UK. In real terms, this means an increase from 2.10 million businesses to 2.16 million businesses. ONS figures also state that 89 per cent of all businesses have less than ten employees and 32 per cent of businesses were less than four years old. So the importance of small- and medium-sized businesses to the UK economy cannot be overstated.

When you consider the significance of small- and medium-sized enterprise, you will appreciate why it is vital that you come to understand the key ideas and theories that surround business enterprise.

In Chapter 1 you will learn about the following areas:

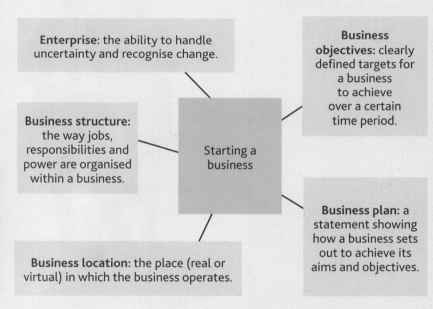

Enterprise: the ability to handle uncertainty and recognise change.

Business objectives: clearly defined targets for a business to achieve over a certain time period.

Business structure: the way jobs, responsibilities and power are organised within a business.

Starting a business

Business plan: a statement showing how a business sets out to achieve its aims and objectives.

Business location: the place (real or virtual) in which the business operates.

What is business?

A **business** is an organisation that is set up to provide goods or services to customers, such as the public, government or other businesses. Businesses provide this in return for money, with the overall aim of increasing the wealth of the owners.

There are a number of different types of business: those that are run by just one single person; those that are run by two or more partners; those that are owned by 'shareholders' (a term you will learn more about later); and those that are run for a range of reasons, whether to make money or simply to help others. In this Unit you will learn about all these types of businesses.

Why start a business?

There are a variety of reasons why people start their own businesses – these are outlined in Diagram **A**.

Objectives

Understand what a business is.

Understand the reasons for starting a business.

Key terms

Business: an activity that requires the organisation of resources to achieve a reward, whilst running a risk.

Entrepreneur: an individual with an idea for a business.

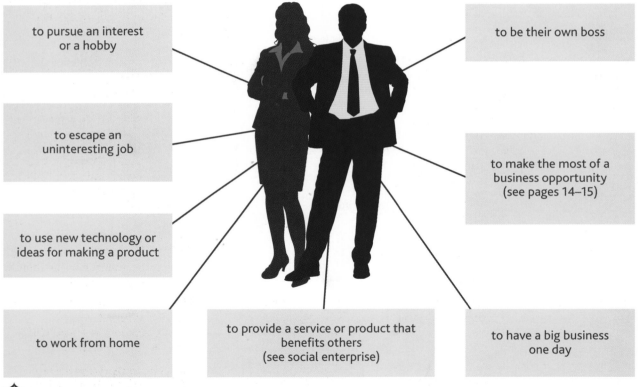

to pursue an interest or a hobby

to escape an uninteresting job

to use new technology or ideas for making a product

to work from home

to provide a service or product that benefits others (see social enterprise)

to be their own boss

to make the most of a business opportunity (see pages 14–15)

to have a big business one day

A *Reasons for starting a business*

Individuals who start their own businesses are known as **entrepreneurs**. So what does it take to be an entrepreneur? Have another look at the entrepreneurs that you met in the Unit opener in 'Meet the entrepreneurs'. Does anything about them surprise you?

What is social enterprise?

Enterprise is about using ideas and related activities to gain a reward such as profit (the money you earn when your income is higher than your costs). However, for some entrepreneurs profit is not enough motivation to persuade them to take the risk and put in place the necessary resources to carry out the activity. Some entrepreneurs need other motivation, such as the belief that they are doing something for their community or for the good of others in society, or even the world! These people are known as 'social entrepreneurs' and they are involved in **social enterprise**.

Nilesh, who you read about in the Unit opener, is an example of a social entrepreneur. He felt the need to do something for the elderly in his community as well as earn some money, so he combined his skills as a decorator with this motivation to set up his decorating business.

> 66 *In my view, social enterprise is the new British business success story, forging a new frontier of enterprise – a quiet revolution involving 55,000 social enterprises in our country from the smallest community groups to larger businesses.* 99
>
> Gordon Brown, then Chancellor of the Exchequer, 15 November 2006

Fifteen

Case study

Award winning chef Jamie Oliver set up his restaurant Fifteen in 2002 to provide disadvantaged young people with the change to gain vocational catering skills and to help them get into the workplace. Since its launch, Fifteen's kitchens have trained close to 100 young chefs and are now planning to partner with other organisations to offer training in related areas in the food service industry. As one of the first celebrity social entrepreneurs, Jamie is keen to expand the contribution Fifteen makes to the future of disadvantaged young people in the UK.

Activities

1 What motivated Jamie Oliver to set up his restaurant business Fifteen?

2 What makes this an example of social enterprise?

Business is all about people making ideas happen to achieve a range of rewards, not just for themselves but also for others. However, there is always a risk as well as a reward attached to every idea.

Activities

3 Review the reasons for setting up a business. What reasons would you have for setting up in business? Would you want to help others with your business?

Review the entrepreneurs you read about in the Unit opener.

4 Why did these people want to start a business?

5 What resources would each entrepreneur need?

Key terms

Social enterprise: an activity that achieves a reward for society.

B Nilesh is a social entrepreneur

Research activity 📁

According to **www.startups.co.uk** the top five business heroes in the UK are:

- Richard Branson
- Steve Jobs
- Anita Roddick
- Stavros
- Duncan Bannatyne

Try to find out about these entrepreneurs and their inspiration for starting up businesses.

∞ **links**

Read about young entrepreneurs at **www.youngbizuk.co.uk**

Find out why Anita Roddick set up The Body Shop at **www.youtube.com** (search for 'Anita Roddick interview').

AQA Examiner's tip

When writing about enterprise in the exam, be sure to explain that it means more than just traditional business ideas; it can include social enterprise too.

1.2   Finding a gap in the market

■ Business opportunities

Every business begins with an opportunity identified by an individual or a group of people. For most entrepreneurs this opportunity is a way of making money for themselves by producing a product or providing a service, and by finding a **gap in the market**. However, for social entrepreneurs this may be also a way of helping or providing for others.

However, it is not enough to provide the same product or service that other businesses are offering; after all why would customers choose your business? What some businesses do is to make themselves different to the competition in some way, such as by providing excellent customer service. Another alternative is to identify a new idea and then turn this into a business opportunity by organising the resources required. Of course, one of the greatest challenges is finding that new idea.

■ Market observation

Learning from the world around them is an important way entrepreneurs identify new business ideas. They watch what happens between existing businesses and their customers and try to identify ways they could do the same thing slightly differently or better. They might also look at investing in existing business ideas, such as franchises (see pages 16–17), where an existing business has an idea but has decided to expand by inviting others to invest in their business.

Entrepreneurs can employ creative-thinking techniques to identify new ideas. They may take an existing product or service and try and look at it in different ways. Gü puddings that we now see on the shelves of all the major UK supermarkets came about because James Averdeick, Gü's founder, spent some time in Belgium enjoying the chocolate from his local bakery, so much so he believed that chocolate lovers in the UK 'needed' to enjoy puddings of a similar quality. Gü chocolate puddings were launched in the UK in 2003. Its website estimates that a Gü pudding is eaten somewhere in the world every two seconds.

Key terms

Gap in the market: a business opportunity that is either a completely new idea or adds something different to an existing product or service.

A   Gü puddings

Activities

1. Working in small groups, choose an everyday product with which you are all familiar and think about ways it could be improved.

2. Identify an everyday product or service with which you are familiar. Identify a number of companies that sell it. How do they make themselves different from each other to win our custom?

Market mapping

Market mapping is one way in which business can find 'gaps' in the market – in other words, identify business opportunities that are not currently being pursued. You need to identify the key attribute or variable of similar products or services in their market. For example, for shoes this may be price and purpose. People tend to buy shoes according to the purpose they serve and the price that is being charged. You then construct a two-dimensional diagram plotting all the current makes of shoe on the market in relation to the characteristics. Jimmy Choo, for example, are very expensive shoes and are all about luxury rather than necessarily being functional. Therefore they appear high on the price axis and closer to luxury on the purpose axis.

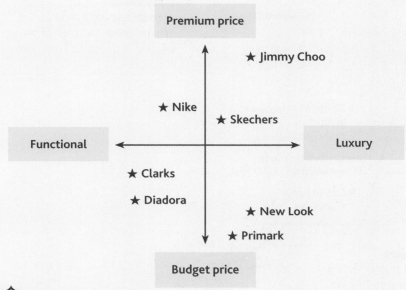

B *Market mapping*

Once all the current products are mapped it may become clear where there is a gap in the market, in other words a space on the map where no products currently exist. The next question is whether that gap can be transformed into a business opportunity.

C *Jimmy Choo shoes are a luxury product*

⚭links

Think of some business ideas using a range of creative-thinking games. Search for 'creative thinking activities and games' at: www.google.com

Did you know ??????

Business opportunities don't need to be completely brand new, but can simply be created by looking at the world around us in a different way.

Research activity

Identify the competitors for a business with which you are familiar – can you construct a market map to identify if there are any gaps in the market?

Find that idea

Investing into a **franchise** is a relatively quick way for an entrepreneur to start a business. An existing business will have developed a considerable amount of knowledge and expertise around the business idea and be looking for people to buy the right to use that idea in return for a share in the profits. Many businesses are operated as franchises; McDonald's outlets in the UK are largely franchised operations.

Objectives

Understand the concept of a franchise.

Understand advantages and disadvantages of operating as a franchise.

Key terms

Franchise: the legal right to use the name and logo of an existing firm and sell the same products.

Advantages	Disadvantages
• Able to sell an already recognised and successful product	
• Take advantage of experience of franchisor	• Some of revenue is paid to franchisor
• Benefit from central services such as marketing and training	• Lacks complete ownership
	• Could lose franchise

A *Weighing up risk and reward*

B *McDonald's is franchised in the UK*

Taking on a franchise is an option worth considering for anyone who wants to run a business but doesn't have a specific business idea or would like to minimise the risk of setting up in business.

The right franchise can give you a head start. Instead of setting up a business from scratch, you use a proven business idea. Typically, you trade under the brand name of the business offering you the franchise, and it also gives you help and support. You will have access to guidance on how to run the business and often benefit from the company's national or even international marketing strategy. In return, you will be typically expected to pay an initial fee and then a share of your profits to the franchisor.

Successful franchises have a much lower failure rate than completely new businesses. However, you will still need to work hard to make the franchise a success and you may have to sacrifice some of your own business ideas to fit in with the franchisor's terms.

In 2003 it was estimated that there were approximately 34,000 operating franchisees turning over £9.65 billion. Of these, almost 97 per cent had made a profit within five years, compared to 45 per cent of other independent business (British Franchise Association).

Activities

1 What are the benefits of buying a franchise for someone who wants to run their own business?

2 Are there any disadvantages associated with franchise ownership?

3 What type of business would make a successful franchise?

Did you know ??????

Buying a franchise can offer someone who wants to run their own business an opportunity to invest in a tried and tested business idea.

links

Find out more at:

www.TheUKFranchiseDirectory.net

www.whichfranchise.com

Case study

Taotalk goes silent

When Alexi Meisl set up his mobile phone company Taotalk, he had no idea that in such a short time his business was going to fail. Initially everything looked good – he found a great shop location, had agreed reasonable contracts with his suppliers and sales were satisfactory. Alexi had also reached the position where he was employing a dozen staff. Taotalk was anything but silent. However, Alexi's plans were to grow the business as quickly as possible, and for this he needed to find finance to enable him to invest in more new shops and buy the stock required.

Once again, everything looked favourable. Alexi had found an investor who was willing to invest a significant sum of money into the business in return for a share in the ownership of the business. However, just before Alexi was going to sign the lease agreement to rent a number of new shop premises, the investor changed his mind and advised Alexi that he was no longer willing to invest in Taotalk. Consequently, Alexi was unable to expand the business as he had planned and eventually the business failed.

The good news is that Alexi is already back in business, but this time with a business partner who is willing to share the risk and the reward.

C Taotalk mobile phones

Activities

4 How could Alexi have reduced the level of risk for Taotalk?

5 How could Alexi have benefited from franchising his business idea?

1.4 Business objectives

All businesses have **aims** and **objectives**. Business objectives do not always remain constant, but are often reviewed and revised as the business matures. A start-up business (one that is about to or has just started trading) may have a different set of objectives from an established successful business. For example, when learning a sport you have to think very carefully about every part of the game, but as you become more experienced you can concentrate on the parts of the game you find most difficult and improving your performance. The same is true for businesses. When a business is starting up there are certain things on which it must concentrate:

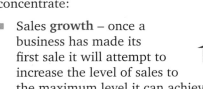

A *Achieving that target!*

- Sales **growth** – once a business has made its first sale it will attempt to increase the level of sales to the maximum level it can achieve.

- Making a **profit** – this is typically measured both as an amount of profit (e.g. £3,000 profit) or as a percentage (e.g. 10 per cent profit), which is known as the **profit margin**.

- Survival – keeping the business open is likely to be one of the most important objectives in the first years of trading. A business will only survive if sufficient **sales** are being made to cover its costs. Otherwise it will need to borrow money to cover costs, which, ultimately, it may not be able to repay.

- **Market share** – depending on the number and type of competitors the business faces, it will have control of a share of the total market (normally expressed as a percentage). For example, Cola-Cola and Pepsi each have almost 50 per cent of the total market for cola. Achieving a greater market share is a common objective for business.

- **Customer satisfaction** – achieving high levels of customer satisfaction will not only result positively in terms of sales, but also in terms of customer loyalty, repeat business and word-of-mouth advertising.

- Social objectives – for a social entrepreneur these may be either to make enough money to share with others, or for the business itself to provide a product or service that helps others. Alternatively, for profit-making businesses, there is the need to consider their business **ethics**. Taking into account the effect the business has on others may also affect profit, as customers may not be willing to buy from it if it is unethical.

We will look at the objectives that more mature and experienced businesses set themselves in later chapters.

It is vital for a business to set itself objectives, and to monitor and review these objectives to ensure that it will achieve its overall aims.

Objectives

Understand the range of objectives that a small business might have.

Understand the purpose of setting objectives.

Key terms

Business aim: a stated target for the future. For example, a new business may have the aim to survive its first year of trading.

Business objective: a clearly defined target for a business to achieve over a certain period of time.

Growth: an increase in turnover (sales), market share or profit.

Profit: what is left after costs have been deducted from revenue.

$$Profit = revenue - costs$$

Profit margin: profit made as a proportion of sales revenue.

Sales: the amount sold or the value sold (e.g. 200 units or £400).

Market share: the proportion of total market sales sold by one business.

Customer satisfaction: how happy the customer is with the product or service.

Ethics: the moral questions on which decisions are made and the impact the business has on its internal and external environment.

Case study

Beauty Rooms

Vicky Narwan set up Beauty Rooms in 2006, providing beauty treatments such as threading, waxing, manicures, pedicures, facials and eyelash tinting. Vicky had always wanted to be self-employed, and so when she and her husband decided to start a family, she knew this would be an opportunity to work for herself at times that would fit in with her family life. She set herself clear objectives for the first year of trading:

- Recruit enough clients to cover the initial costs of setting up the business.

- Increase awareness of Beauty Rooms' services by providing an excellent level of service and asking clients to recommend her business.

Vicky was not too concerned about making a profit in her first year as she was also working part-time for another business, which guaranteed her an income.

B *Beauty Rooms*

Activities

1. Why was it important for Vicky to set objectives for her business?

2. Why was Vicky concerned about recruiting enough clients to cover the initial costs of setting up the business?

3. Identify two new objectives that Vicky might set herself when she becomes wholly self-employed.

Research activity

Find out about the objectives of some local businesses. Have these changed since they started trading?

Activity

4. Have a go at setting some objectives. Think about your Business Studies course and set yourself an objective for the end of the course. This might be related to a particular grade you want to achieve or to the knowledge or skills that you would like to acquire. Who do you think you should share this objective with? Who might help you achieve it? Write the objective down in your notes now so you can refer to it throughout your course.

■ Clear objectives

A business that sets itself objectives is able to work towards something. Have you ever been set an objective to work towards? Maybe at school or college your teacher has suggested you might achieve a certain grade if you keep working hard, or your parent or carer might have offered you a reward if you keep your room tidy for a week? Objectives can take many forms, but above all they must be clear.

There is no point in setting objectives that people don't understand as they will not know what they are supposed to be doing. In some ways it is just as important that people understand the *reason* for the objective. Did your parent or carer explain *why* you need to keep your room tidy? If you had realised it was because they were worried your younger brother or sister might damage your things, would you have made more of an effort? So objectives need to be understood by everyone, and sharing the reason for the objective can help this.

AQA *Examiner's tip*

When writing about business objectives, remember that businesses may have different objectives at different stages of their growth.

A Success can come in many forms

Business success

In the previous pages we considered business objectives: the targets set by businesses to direct their actions. Commonly, profit or **turnover** is a business's main objective. Profit is calculated by deducting the costs from revenue (sales). A business works out the total of all its costs, such as raw materials, staff salaries, rent, and so on. It then calculates how much revenue it earned from the sales of its product or service. The final calculation deducts (subtracts) the costs from the revenue, giving the profit or loss.

Key term

Turnover: the value of sales made during a trading period, also called revenue.

| Profit | = | Revenue | – | Cost |

If a business achieves these objectives they could be considered successful. For example, for Ania's gardening business, her most important objective was to find 50 customers in the first year, which would enable her to earn enough money to cover her costs and pay herself a salary. At the end of the year, Ania could judge her success by recording how many customers she had found in that year. If the number was 50 or more, she had been successful.

B Ania's business objectives are vital to her chances of success

However, if Ania had only found 48 customers in that first year, would that mean she had failed? Yes, she had failed to meet that objective, but, as outlined on page 18, a key objective for a start-up business is survival. If 48 customers was enough for Ania to keep the business going, then maybe overall we could say that Ania had been successful in her first year. Each individual objective is important to a business, but it must also look at the objectives more broadly, continually questioning them. Maybe some of Ania's 48 customers actually bought more from her than she had anticipated, so overall her level of sales was higher than she expected. If so, does the number of customers really matter?

Case study

PJ's Disco

Pete and Jane set up their mobile disco to try and increase their family income: both worked full time in other jobs but had always enjoyed music and making people laugh! In their first year of running the business they weren't concerned about how many bookings they made, as they wanted to concentrate on developing their service. They wanted to ensure that their customers were happy and gather feedback about how their service could be improved.

After the first year of trading, once they were confident they knew what they were doing, they set themselves an objective of one booking per week. By the end of the first six months of the second year they were achieving on average two bookings per week but Jane wasn't happy. They had very little time to enjoy their own lives as they were both constantly working.

Activities

2 Would you consider this business to be successful? Explain your answer.

3 How could Pete and Jane change their objectives to improve their success?

Activity

1 Objectives can be used to measure success such as making a profit.

Look back at the entrepeneurs and consider which of the other objectives would help to measure their success.

AQA Examiner's tip

When answering a question about measuring success remember to consider **all** possible objectives – not just profit.

∞ links

Research small businesses at: www.uksmallbusinessdirectory.co.uk

Did you know ??????

Setting clear business objectives is vital to business success.

Research activity

Identify a small business in your area or on the internet. Can you find out what their objectives are for this year? How will they monitor whether those objectives have been met?

1.6 Business objectives: stakeholders

In Business objectives: measuring success (pages 20–1) we learnt how business owners use objectives to measure their success. However, is it just the business owner that judges whether a business has been successful? Do you think other people who are affected by the business should also have a say?

Objectives

Consider how stakeholders can influence business objectives.

Activity

1 Review the circumstances of Nilesh, from 'Meet the entrepreneurs' in the Unit opener. Who do you think his business affects?

Stakeholders

Stakeholders are individuals or groups with an interest in a business. The level of interest of each stakeholder group depends upon the type of business. For example, Alex's web design business (see 'Meet the entrepreneurs' in the Unit opener) has very little impact on his local community as he works from his home office, and in fact most of his neighbours do not even realise he has a business. However, a company such as British Nuclear Fuels, which runs all Britain's nuclear power stations, has a big impact on the communities where power stations are based because of the potentially hazardous nature of their work.

Key terms

Stakeholder: an individual or group with an interest in a business, such as employees, customers, managers, shareholders, suppliers, competitors and the local community.

Activity

2 Identify a business with which you are familiar and create a spider diagram to identify the business's stakeholders.

A Business stakeholders

■ Stakeholder influence

So stakeholders will have an opinion on whether the business is successful, because if they have been positively or negatively affected by the business, they will judge it accordingly. For example, if Alex's web design clients start visiting him at his home office and parking all along the road, his neighbours may be unhappy with this. However, it is up to Alex, as the business owner, to consider whether this stakeholder group's judgement of his business matters. If he believes it does matter, this group of stakeholders will affect the way Alex does business. He may choose to find an office away from home in a business park or other suitable location.

Activity

3 Return to the spider diagram you created earlier and add some notes to describe how each stakeholder group affects the business's activities and objectives.

Group activity

Role play a meeting of business stakeholders for one of the 'Meet the entrepreneurs' businesses (see Unit opener). Debate whose needs are most important. For example, are the needs of the customers more important than the needs of the employees?

Did you know ??????

A business needs to consider its stakeholders when setting its objectives as they may affect the business's ability to meet those objectives.

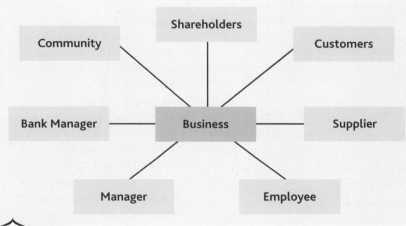

B Business stakeholders

Stakeholders can have a considerable influence on the way a business carries out its activities and consequently its ability to meet its objectives.

Agenda

Date & time: 13 June 2009

Location: Reception room 4

Present: CEO, Dept heads

Apologies: Finance director, Jim Cash

Item 1: Role of each stakeholder

Item 2: Importance of each stakeholder to business

Item 3: Impact of each stakeholder on business

Vote: Order stakeholders in priority to business

Any other business:

C A business meeting agenda should be presented in a clear and simple manner

1.7　Business plans

Why plan?

Ever been on a car journey when someone claims, 'I know where it is! We don't need a map,' and then spent several stressful hours driving around in circles? A business plan is like a map. You know where you need to get to, but a map is a very useful tool in getting you there by the shortest, least stressful route. In a similar way, a business may know its objectives but needs a plan of how it is going to achieve them.

As well as achieving its objectives, a business wants to ensure it achieves them in the most efficient, cost-saving and profitable way. Having a plan assists a business to identify its costs, organise its resources, calculate its turnover and anticipate any risks.

A **business plan** typically includes a number of sections:

- Mission/aims – states the goal of the business.
- Objectives – states what needs to be done to achieve the goal.
- Market environment – considers what is happening around the business that will affect it.
- Competition – how many competitors there are and what they are doing.
- Product/service – a description of what the business is offering.
- Marketing – how the business plans to let potential customers know about its product/service.
- Distribution – how the business plans to get its product to the customer.
- **Funding** – how much all this is going to cost.
- **Forecasts** – how much money the business expects to earn.
- Resources – what resources the business currently has available and what it needs in the future.
- Timescale – when it is all going to happen.

A　*With a map you are more likely to reach your destination!*

Activities

1　So now you understand the purpose of a business plan, what does one look like? Have a look at Alex's business plan opposite to identify the key sections within a business plan.

2　Minseung didn't write a business plan when she started her business. Why do you think this was? How might this affect her business?

Alex's business plan

Mission/aims
The development of professional, yet affordable websites and related services for small and medium enterprises.

Objectives
- To generate £50,000 sales in Year 1.
- To achieve a profit margin of 55 per cent by the end of Year 2.
- To be recognised as the leading web developer within the UK for small and medium enterprises by Year 5.

Market environment
Highly competitive with a number of large- and small-scale competitors with a wide range of expertise and pricing to match.
New web developers are joining the market all the time and equally existing web developers are failing and leaving the market. A highly changeable market environment, but there is huge growth potential working with small and medium enterprises as they realise that customers expect them to be on the internet and do not have the expertise to develop their own websites.

Competition
Many competitors are based nationally and locally, but having analysed the products, services and pricing of each there is real potential for an affordably priced business that understands the needs of small and medium enterprises.

Product/service
- Basic website design
- Website hosting
- Website maintenance and management
- E-commerce

Marketing
- We will have our own website to market our services, which will be constructed in such a way that it will be ranked highly by search engines such as Google, Yahoo and so on.
- *We will also advertise in electronic versions of Yellow Pages, Thompson Local* and other business directories.
- We will ask clients for testimonials and recommendations.
- We will attend all relevant trade fairs to demonstrate our services.

Distribution
Not applicable.

Funding and forecasts
See cash flow and profit and loss forecasts for Years 1–5.

Resources
- Apple PowerBook
- Hewlett Packard Servers for hosting
- Home office equipment

Timescale
- Company website currently under development – will be completed by end of month.
- Recruit first clients within two months.
- Attend trade shows in spring and summer.

∞ links

For a useful presentation on business plans created by business advisers 'Wisteria' visit **www.wisteria.co.uk** (click on business tips & tools>How to create an effective Business Plan).

More guidance is available from Business Link, a national network of free business advice and support. Visit **www.businesslink.gov.uk**

■ Risk versus reward

There is always **risk** and reward associated with business and we have considered the fact that entrepreneurs need to decide if the reward is worth the risk before embarking on their business start-up. One of the ways in which an entrepreneur can try and deal with risk is to first identify it and then put plans in place to try and either remove it completely or reduce its impact on the business.

General business risks

- **Business failure** – complete closure or even bankruptcy.
- **Partial business failure** – closure of certain parts (divisions) of the business.
- **Loss of earnings** – for the owner and/or employees.
- **Shrinking market** – reduction in the number of potential customers and the subsequent impact on sales.
- **Loss of market share** – competition takes some of the business's customers.
- **Personal risks** – to finance, relationships and even health.

Functional risks

- **Marketing** – the market research data is incorrect and consequently wrong decisions are made.
- **Sales** – customers' incomes change and they can no longer afford to buy the product.
- **Operations** – a competitor sources new technology, which means it is more efficient than the business.
- **Finance** – interest rates increase, which means the bank loan costs far more per month.
- **Human resources** – unable to recruit anyone locally with the right skills.

■ Business uncertainty

Even though the entrepreneur may have written a business plan and tried to identify all the risks that a business might face, there is nothing certain in business. **Uncertainty** arises when we are unable to identify or forecast what is going to happen. Having read the Taotalk case study on page 17, you will remember that Alexi thought that investment promised by his investor was certain, but ultimately that proved not to be the case and caused the failure of Alexi's business.

Business uncertainty can be a real source of stress and anxiety for entrepreneurs and unfortunately little can be done about it – there is no entrepreneurial crystal ball! For an entrepreneur and their business to deal with uncertainty, they must proceed with caution and develop a business that is flexible, which can deal with change. For example, if Alexi had not relied solely on this one investor, but identified a number of alternatives, it would have enabled him to deal with the withdrawal of that one investor.

Key terms

Risk: the potential for loss but rewards in business make it a calculated gamble.

Uncertainty: not knowing the future, or what is going to happen.

A *There is no entrepreneurial crystal ball!*

B   *The start-up of a business is the beginning of the challenge!*

∞ links

Read about how Cadbury
Schweppes considers its risks.
www.investis.com/
cadburyschweppes/reports/
anr2005/db/risk.html

Activity

1   Uncertainty in business is difficult to anticipate by its very nature. Read through Alex's business plan on page 25. Can you identify what uncertainties and risks they might face? For example, Alex could be uncertain about how he is going to actually recruit his first customers – will his marketing do its job?

■ Planning for uncertainty

As you learnt earlier, a business plan seeks to set out how a business is going to achieve its aims and objectives. However, a business plan needs to do more than that – it needs to attempt to identify what might happen in the future and show how the business will deal with that. For example, a business that is not certain whether there will be enough customers in its geographical area may explore other areas and identify them in its plan as having potential for the future. Equally, a business that is not certain about the costs of its materials may decide to agree a fixed price with its suppliers; this may be slightly higher than the normal price but is guaranteed.

Activity

2   Look at the list of uncertainties you identified Nilesh and Alex might face. Try to identify how they could deal with each uncertainty. What plans could they put in place?

By considering alternatives, also known as contingencies, a business plan is strengthened. However, we must be aware that no business plan is perfect. Events happen that cannot be foreseen and the business world is constantly changing. This means that business plans should not just be written and left in a drawer gathering dust, they should be a 'living' document, which should be continually revisited and updated to reflect changes taking place and new challenges ahead.

> **Did you know ??????**
>
> Flexibility and contingency planning are key to the ability of a business to deal with risk and uncertainty.

1.9 Legal structure: sole trader and partnership

Which is the right legal structure?

Choosing the right legal structure is probably one of the first decisions you need to make as an entrepreneur, particularly if the idea and enthusiasm for the business is not yours alone. It is important to clarify exactly who will be taking the risks and sharing in the rewards.

It is also important for a number of other reasons, such as:

- how much tax and National Insurance the business pays
- which records and accounts have to be kept
- who is liable (responsibility) for the business's debt and up to how much
- what sources of finance are available to the business
- who has control of the business and therefore makes the decisions.

There are a number of options open to businesses in terms of their legal structure. The first two we will consider are sole trader and partnership.

Sole trader

The simplest form of business is typically an individual operating alone – a **sole trader**. However, a sole trader can actually employ people and still be classified as a sole trader. The important fact is that the responsibility for the business lies with the individual – they are responsible for keeping basic records for tax and national insurance purposes.

Partnership

In a **partnership** two or more people (maximum 20) share risks, costs and responsibilities. The partners take a share in the profits and a share in the decision-making, although this might not be an equal share. The partners are, however, jointly responsible for any debts and if one of the partners leave then the partnership must be dissolved.

A *Equal partners share the decision-making*

Objectives

Be aware of the different forms of small business ownership: sole traders and partnerships.

Understand the benefits and limitations of sole traders and partnerships.

Understand what is meant by limited liability.

Key terms

Sole trader: the most common form of business organisation, often just one person.

Partnership: the simplest way two or more people can be in business together where partners are jointly and personally responsible for debts.

Unlimited liability: unincorporated businesses, such as sole traders and partnerships, have unlimited liability, which means that the owners are responsible for all the business's debts.

⚭ links

For more information about incorporated businesses, take a look at pages 30–1.

Did you know ??????

Sole traders do not necessarily work alone – they just take sole responsibility for risk and reward.

Sole traders and partnerships have unlimited liability – they take personal responsibility for all the debts of the business.

B *Benefits and drawbacks of sole trader and partnership structures*

Type of structure	Benefits	Drawbacks
Sole trader	Simple and quick to set up.	**Unlimited liability** for owner.
	Inexpensive to set up.	Raising additional finance can be difficult due to individual's limited resources.
	Profit kept by owner.	Decisions all made by owner who may not have specific expertise.
	Owner has complete control of business.	Reliant on health and wellbeing of owner.
	Hours of work can be tailored to suit the business owner.	
Partnership	Very few procedures to set up.	Unlimited liability for owners.
	Expertise of a number of people combined.	Profits are shared amongst owners.
	More sources of finance as more people are involved.	Decisions of other partners must be honoured.
		Maximum of 20 people can join the partnership.
		Partnership ends when one partner leaves.

Activity

1 Do you enjoy working alone or would you prefer the support of others? Consider whether you would be best suited to being a sole trader or partnership.

Case study

Deli 28

University student, Hannah Pursall, set up Deli 28 in 2007, realising that she could make significant improvements to the type of business she worked in whilst on work placement.

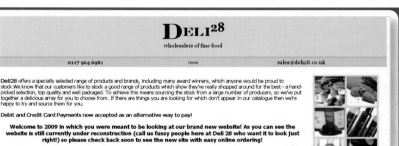

C *Deli 28*

Deli 28 is a wholesaler of fine foods that sells to retailers and to businesses involved in food production, such as delicatessens, restaurants, sandwich shops and hotels. When considering setting up the business, Hannah had to consider the right legal structure for the business. As a sole trader Hannah would be solely responsible for the debts of the business, but also she would be the only recipient of the profit. She was aware that setting up her business as a sole trader would enable her to get started quickly with only a minimum requirement to keep records for basic tax, National Insurance and Value Added Tax (VAT) purposes. However, although a partnership may take a little longer to set up, Hannah would not be solely responsible for the risks, costs and responsibilities of the business.

Ultimately, Hannah felt that the sole trader option was the best route for her. After all, she was the one who had the idea for the business and the enthusiasm to see it through. It was also true that Hannah wouldn't be working alone, as a number of her family had agreed to work for her on a part-time basis to support her. This would enable her not only to have day-to-day help, but also colleagues with whom she could discuss important decisions.

Activities

2 Why do you think Hannah chose the sole trader option?

3 What benefits would she have gained if she took the partnership option?

1.10 Legal structure: limited and unlimited

Sole traders and partnerships, are both examples of unincorporated businesses, unlike private limited companies, which are incorporated. **Incorporation** means that the business exists legally. If the business incurs any debts, these debts belong to the business and not the owners, so the owners have **limited liability**. Table **A** illustrates these points.

Research activity

1 What would you call your business? Use **www.companieshouse.gov.uk** to see if this name has already been registered.

A *Legal structure, incorporation and liability*

Legal structure	Incorporation	Liability
Sole trader	Unincorporated	Unlimited liability
Partnership	Unincorporated	Unlimited liability
Private limited company	Incorporated	Limited liability

For a sole trader or partnership, the decision to become incorporated offers protection from some of the risks associated with business ownership. If the business fails the owner's personal belongings (assets) will be unaffected. However, the incorporation process is complicated and requires the owners to keep much more detailed records.

The owners of a limited company are known as shareholders. They each own a proportion of the total shares of the business. The proportion is normally determined by the amount each person has invested in the business. For example, if John invests £20,000 and Mohammad invests £80,000, then it is likely that John will have 20 per cent of the shares and Mohammad will have 80 per cent. Shares in private limited companies can only be sold privately with the agreement of the shareholder.

B *Incorporated companies must register with Companies House*

Objectives

Understand how incorporation enables a business to expand.

Be aware of issues relating to ownership and control.

Key terms

Incorporation: the process of forming a limited liability company such as a private limited company or plc.

Limited liability: investors (shareholders) in a limited company can only lose their investment in the business if it fails; they cannot be forced to sell assets to pay off the firm's debts.

Research activity

2 Have a look on the Companies House website **www.companieshouse. gov.uk** to find out how a business becomes incorporated.

■ Management conflict

Offering ownership to new investors by the owning of shares brings with it an additional challenge. With ownership comes a degree of control and an influence in the decision-making of the business. This can bring new ideas and expertise into the business, but it can also cause conflict if the original business owner disagrees with the new investors.

This can also have an impact on the management of the business. Through the process of business growth, it is likely that the owners will appoint a management team to deal with the day-to-day needs of the business. The separation of ownership from daily management can improve performance as the management team may view the business in a more objective way. However, this can also cause conflict if the management team and owners disagree about the way the business is being run.

The growth of an organisation and the opportunities and challenges it brings will be explored in more detail in Unit 2, but at this stage it is important that you realise that with growth comes real challenges that an entrepreneur may not always welcome.

∞ links

Further information about business expansion can be found from Chapter 6 onwards.

Activity

1   On a large piece of paper, create a table or a spider diagram to illustrate the following types of legal structure, and identify the benefits and drawbacks of each.

a   Sole trader

b   Partnership

c   Private limited company

Did you know ??????

Simply because the business chooses one structure when it starts trading, does not mean it must always remain in that same structure. Typically, when businesses grow they change structure to accommodate their changing needs.

BeGo Coaching and Training

Entrepreneur Tim Hall set up his business as a sole trader – to begin with, his business was simply involved in the coaching and training that he could offer. However, after a number of successful years, Tim was involving freelance trainers who were not employed full time by him but worked for him on a number of large contracts. As time went on, Tim realised he needed some support to help run the business and this is when he approached one of the most-talented freelancers to consider joining him as a partner in the business.

Case study

Activities

2   What should Tim consider when setting up a partnership?

3   What would be the advantages of remaining as a sole trader?

Case study

We do like to work beside the seaside

When Shona Munro looks out of her office window she can see all the way down the valley to the waters of Loch Lomond. Munro is among a growing number of entrepreneurs who are taking advantage of **technology** and communication links to start up their businesses exactly where they choose.

Munro, 35, started up her card design company, Tartan 2CV, in the grounds of her parents' Scottish farm five years ago. Her company now deals with retailers throughout the world and last year had sales of £150,000.

She says: 'I don't think my customers even realise where I am. Once people get you on the end of the phone or send you an email you could just as easily be a huge factory in the middle of a Glasgow industrial estate.'

'And there have been huge financial advantages because I am not having to rent big-city premises.'

The Sunday Times, 19 October 2003

Activities

1. What are the benefits to Tartan 2CV's location?

2. Are there any disadvantages to its location?

Objectives

Consider the factors that influence where a business sets up and operates.

Key terms

Technology: in relation to business location, this refers to the use of e-technology, such as the internet and e-mail, to create a virtual market between the business and the consumer.

Logistics: the process of buying, managing and delivering goods, from the point of manufacture to the end consumer.

■ Location, location, location

There are many factors that affect where a business locates but ultimately the decision rests with the business owners and management. However, in deciding where to locate the business they must prioritise the needs of their stakeholders (see section 1.6). For example, if being too far from customers means the business will struggle to arrange its **logistics** efficiently, then proximity to customers is a key priority. Alternatively, if the business needs staff with particular skills who tend to live in one geographical area (e.g. Silicon Valley in California or the City in London), then the business may have to locate close to its staff.

B   *Where is it best to locate your business?*

Costs
Rent or buy?
Impact on business image?
Cost of utilities.
Transportation costs.
Wage levels in area.
Cost of sourcing materials.

Infrastructure
Transport links for goods in and goods out.
Access for staff and customers.
Availability of local services.

Factors affecting business location

The market
How near to customer/ competition.

Other factors
Entrepreneur's lifestyle choices.
Planning laws.
Subsidies, government and local council initiatives.
Availability of premises.

A   *Factors affecting business location*

The internet factor

It is predicted that by 2018 internet shopping could account for half of Britain's £300 billion a year retail shopping **market**. The phenomenal upsurge in the use of the internet by consumers has forced businesses to think about the way in which they sell their products and services. For some businesses it has proved a real challenge to find alternative ways to get their products to their online and **mail-order** customers.

For many businesses, particularly small- and medium-sized businesses, this has been an excellent opportunity to compete with larger, more established competitors. For example, if your customer is shopping via your website, do they care whether you have a store on Oxford Street or in Birmingham's Bull Ring? No, they simply want the same product at the best price, and ideally delivered to their door. Dell Computers is an excellent example of a business that has maximised sales via the internet by choosing not to incur the costs associated with setting up retail shops.

C *Dell Computers has reduced its costs by choosing not to have their own retail outlets*

Key terms

Market: where the buyer and seller 'come together' to exchange the goods or services for money. Today this may not actually mean a face-to-face meeting, but could be carried out over the internet or other telecommunication method.

Mail order: direct marketing through mail shots leading to goods being delivered directly to customer.

Activity

3 In groups, assess your local area in terms of its costs and benefits as a potential business location. You may want to:

- Look at the websites for commercial estate agents and assess availability and costs of business premises.
- Find out from your local council what they do to attract business into the area.
- Do a geographical survey of local infrastructure.
- Talk to a local recruitment agency about the skills of the local workforce.
- Interview local business people about their decision to locate their business in your community.

Did you know ??????

Decisions regarding business location will depend on the nature of the product or service, associated costs, the availability of suitable premises and ultimately the relative importance of the various stakeholder groups.

In this chapter you have learnt:

- ✔ what business and enterprise means and why someone might want to start a business
- ✔ how entrepreneurs find gaps in the market
- ✔ about franchising
- ✔ the importance of objectives in planning and measuring business performance for all stakeholders
- ✔ about the role of business plans and the need to manage risk and uncertainty
- ✔ the different types of legal structure for start-up businesses
- ✔ about the impact of business location.

Revision questions

1 Which of the following is an example of social enterprise?

a Advertising agency

b Computer manufacturer

c Restaurant training young offenders

d Caravan site.

2 Which of the following is an advantage of buying a franchise?

a Make more profit

b Access to a successful business idea

c Lower costs

d Have total control of a business.

3 Which of the following is a benefit of writing a business plan?

a It takes time

b You use a word processor

c You choose what you want to do

d You identify risks.

4 What benefit does limited liability give an entrepreneur?

a More sales

b Access to greater market information

c Reduced number of competitors

d Protection of personal assets.

5 Business location would be important to a bakery because of which of the following?

a Proximity to customers

b Access to local suppliers

c Access to transport infrastructure

d Technology.

6 Which is these is **not** a reason for starting a business?

a To have more time for yourself

b To make a living from something you are interested in doing

c To make money

d To be in control of your own future.

2 Marketing

Marketing is used to describe a range of activities undertaken by a firm in its relationship with its customers or potential customers. Marketing activities include:

- finding out what people want from the firm's product or service
- using this research information to try to make sure the goods and services provided by the business are what consumers want
- pricing the products at the most appropriate levels
- promoting the products in the most appropriate ways
- selling products to customers in the most convenient way to them.

This suggests that marketing is very important, especially for a small business trying to get established.

However, marketing in small businesses is often limited by a lack of money. Small firms generally do not have a vast amount of money to spend on marketing – they will need to keep to a budget when designing and promoting their product.

- Market research will have to be done quickly and cheaply, such as a questionnaire to existing customers.
- Products cannot be developed beyond the resources of the small business – customer service may be more important than the latest and most advanced product.
- Television promotions will probably be out of the question for small firms, but leaflets, local newspaper adverts and the internet are common forms of promotion used by new businesses.

A start-up business will need to market its product well, since it is vital that possible customers know that there is a new product or service available, what it can do for them and how they can buy it.

Make it in films

Andy is an expert in making short films for schools, colleges, business promotions and weddings. Over the last month he only had two calls from possible customers. A friend has advised him to do some marketing to make his film business more successful. The friend suggested:

- finding out which other small business offer the same service in this region
- changing the prices charged – customers might be put off by the £250 minimum charge
- promoting the film service more (Andy depended on posted leaflets to advertise his business).

Activity

Do you agree with Andy's friend that more marketing activities might make Andy's business more succeessful? Explain your answer.

Case study

2.1   Market research with limited budgets

■ Why conduct market research?

History has proved that some businesses succeed based entirely on the entrepreneur's faith in their idea, such as Dyson's vacuum cleaner. However, many more guesses have proved to be foolish, leading new businesses to fail rapidly as the entrepreneurs did not understand exactly what customers wanted, or had not noticed that a direct competitor offered a much better product.

A wise entrepreneur will try to find out a little about his/her market and customers before starting up, by carrying out **market research**.

There are two types of market research: primary research and secondary research.

Primary research is information that has not previously existed before and this is often obtained through field research such as interviewing people face to face, conducting surveys, which can include sending questionnaires to people.

Secondary research, or desk research, relies on gathering information that already exists, either in the company, such as previous sales information, or externally, perhaps from the government or trade associations for example.

Primary research is often the most useful, as it is more up-to-date and specific. Primary research will be very important to a new start-up business, especially as there will be little secondary data for a new business to utilise.

Really smart entrepreneurs will continue researching into their market once the business is running, as consumers' tastes and buying habits often change.

The main benefits to a small business of market research include:

- knowing customers' needs – helping to avoid wasting money on products that will not sell
- estimating likely demand – so that the firm avoids making too few or too many products
- helping the entrepreneur to understand if the market is big enough to make the business a success
- finding out about competitors' location, products and prices – so that these three important areas will benefit from this information.

Be careful!

Not all market research is reliable. The following table shows why research results need to be treated with care.

Objectives

Understand the reasons for market research.

Understand the methods of market research.

Key terms

Market research: research that enables a firm to find out about its market, its customers and its potential customers.

Primary research: gathering new information specifically for the purposes identified by the business.

Secondary research: research that uses information that has already been gathered for another purpose.

A *Reasons for research inaccuracy*

Secondary research	Primary research
Information may be outdated as it may have been collected some time ago. This makes it less accurate than up-to-date information.	Failure to ask enough people may mean that the information collected does not represent the views of typical consumers.
Information may not be exactly what is needed. This is because it was originally collected for another purpose.	Asking too many people of a particular age group or income level may give results that fail to represent the whole market.
Some sources of secondary information may not be reliable. For example, company websites may present biased information.	Poorly designed questionnaires may use suggestive or leading questions, which may encourage people to give a particular answer to certain questions.

The owners of Woodruffs organic cafe spotted a gap in the market, reflective of location and demographic, in 1998 when they opened Britain's first 100 per cent organic cafe in Stroud, Gloucestershire.

Case study

B *Britain's first totally organic cafe filled a gap in the market*

Research activity

Using the internet, try to find out what percentage of the UK population are vegetarians and how many people live within five miles of your local high street. Choose an alternative location and compare the two.

C The Grocer *magazine is an excellent source of research for new retailers in food and drink*

Activities

An entrepreneur plans to start up a vegetarian café for 14–30-year-olds in your local high street. She wants to find out information about this market using small-scale market research.

1 How many people do you suggest she interviews? Explain your answer.

2 List **five** suitable questions that the entrepreneur might ask.

3 Explain why you have chosen these questions.

∞ links

The Market Research Society represents market research companies in the UK. Find out more on its website, which contains a beginner's guide to research: **www.mrs.org.uk**

The Grocer magazine is aimed specifically at grocery retailers. Have a look around its website to gain an understanding of selling through retail shops: **www.the. grocer.magazine.co.uk**

AQA *Examiner's tip*

Don't forget the importance of market research. Any marketing decision taken without some market research could lead to a big error if the business doesn't understand the needs of the people it is trying to sell to.

Market research methods

There are many ways to find out information about a market and possible customers. Some of these methods are cheaper and easier to use than others. It is these that will be most attractive for a small business.

Where to start?

Secondary research tends to be cheaper than primary research – it can take the form of library or internet searches. Secondary research can help to find the right focus for primary research. For example, if an entrepreneur planning to open a café has found out that 50 per cent of all coffee is drunk by those over 50 years old, he is likely to make sure that about 50 per cent of all people he interviews in his area are from this age range, before deciding to open the café.

Therefore, library or internet research should probably be the first thing to do. It can discover a range of information, possibly focused on a local area, or perhaps specialist information on total sales for a certain type of product.

Primary research for small businesses

The easiest, cheapest way to get information from people on how to improve your business is using feedback from existing customers.

This is free of charge, constantly updated and gives valuable information on how to keep current customers satisfied. However, many businesses would love to know the thoughts of people who are not current customers. Knowing why some people have never bought your product or come into your shop, or perhaps why a past customer has stopped using your business, can help to increase customer numbers.

Constructing a questionnaire

Key features of a good questionnaire

Often businesses will give customers a **questionnaire** to complete.

- Most questions should be closed questions. This means that there will only be a few possible answers to each question. This allows the company doing the research to compile and analyse the results more easily. For example, 'Which brand of ice cream do you buy most frequently?'
- A good questionnaire should be as short as possible. This will encourage people to take part in the research and it will make the results easier to analyse.
- Before constructing the questionnaire, research objectives should be set, making clear exactly what the firm wants to discover from the results of the questionnaire. So, if it is important to find out the age range of people who most often buy takeaway pizzas, a question about age should be included.
- Usually the first questions on a questionnaire will establish the type of person being spoken to (age, gender, etc.), which allows

A *Questionnaires are an effective and cheap way of finding out information*

Key terms

Questionnaire: a set of questions designed to discover information relating to a product or service. These may be left for consumers to complete themselves, carried out using face-to-face interviews by researchers or form the basis of a telephone or postal survey.

∞ links

Business Link is a government-funded organisation set up to offer advice to entrepreneurs. Go to its website, select 'Sales and marketing' and explore the advice offered on market research: **www.businesslink.gov.uk**

researchers to stop the questionnaire if the respondent does not fit the sample that the firm wants to find out about.

- Other questions are often used to try to find out the respondent's buying habits and attitudes to the type of product or service being investigated.

Factors a small business should consider

A small business should carefully consider which method(s) to use.

Setting clear research objectives is crucial. Although it might be nice to know why consumers will not pay more than £3 per DVD rental, for a new DVD rental store, knowing that £3 is the limit for most customers may be all they need to know to make their pricing decisions.

Using existing contacts will be cheaper than arranging focus groups. These could provide information on why some consumers spend on some goods and not others, but could take up a lot of time and money.

B *The advantages and disadvantages of the main research methods*

Research methods	Advantages	Disadvantages
Internet research	■ Free of charge. ■ Allow a quick overview of the market.	■ Some sources may be biased (e.g. competitors' websites). ■ Unlikely to be exactly what firm needs to find out.
Telephone survey	■ Cheap. ■ Allows interviewers to clarify any questions that are unclear.	■ May be viewed as a nuisance by those telephoned.
Questionnaire	■ Results are easy to analyse as mostly uses closed questions. ■ A relatively fast way to gather information from a wide range of people.	■ May fail to discover *why* people behave the way they do – just shows how they behave. ■ Interviewer may bias the results through an 'overly-friendly' approach.
Supplier feedback	■ May give insight on future trends, not yet visible 'on the high street'. ■ Helps to build relationships with suppliers.	■ Suppliers may present a biased view.
Customer feedback	■ Real insight as to how to improve the customer experience.	■ Explains nothing about what non-customers think.
Focus group	■ In-depth information about consumer attitudes and motives behind purchasing decisions.	■ Very expensive per person questioned. ■ Only ever carried out on small samples, so the results may be unrepresentative.

Key terms

Internet research: using information that has already been published on the internet to gather information about the market for a firm's products or services.

Telephone survey: a series of set questions delivered over the telephone to consumers as a method of primary research.

Supplier feedback: gathering information from companies that supply products or services on their forecasts for what is likely to happen in the market in the future.

Customer feedback: formal or informal responses from customers to the product or service offered by a business.

Focus group: in-depth discussion with a small group of consumers (8–10), which probes their feelings towards a product or service.

Did you know ??????

It is important to be aware of the limitations imposed by a small budget for research and the choice of method – market research helps to reduce errors, but can never guarantee correct marketing decisions.

Each element of the **marketing mix** requires decisions to be made by a business:

- **Product** – deciding exactly what goods or services are at the heart of a firm's marketing.
- **Price** – what price should be set? Customers may find a low price attractive, but a high price gives more revenue per unit.
- **Promotion** – this enables a firm to let customers know about the product. People who do not know a product is available, or what the product does, will not buy it.
- **Place** – deciding exactly how to get the product to customers.

The marketing mix is also called the 4Ps. Each of these Ps is dealt with in more detail throughout this chapter.

The image of the product and the business

If you had the money, where would you go to buy an Aston Martin car? What's good enough for James Bond will obviously be expensive. To find a dealer selling Aston Martins you will need to go to an exclusive area, such as London's Park Lane. When you get in the car you'll be expecting really comfortable leather seats, luxurious extras and a very fast and well-engineered vehicle. Of course, you will only see these cars advertised where the promotion suggests a classy sophisticated product. When you see the car being promoted, everything you see is likely to try to justify the expensive price tag.

The Aston Martin buying experience demonstrates the need to get all four elements of the marketing mix working together to give off the same image. If Aston Martin started advertising its cars as a cheap and cheerful way to do the shopping by putting small colourful adverts in *The Sun*, the image of the company would be confusing, unless the other Ps were adjusted to suit the new image. A good marketing mix is one where all the 4Ps are giving off the same, clear image about a company's offerings. Small businesses that cut selling prices may find that customers doubt the quality of their products, whilst a low-price retailer based in the richest part of town will struggle to attract the customers it is aimed at.

A *The marketing mix creates an image of quality and sophistication*

Objectives

Understand the elements of the marketing mix.

Understand how a small business could select an appropriate marketing mix.

Key terms

Marketing mix: the four major variables for which decisions must be made when marketing a product.

Product: the service or physical good being sold by the company.

Price: the amount charged by a business for its product or service.

Promotion: all the ways a business communicates to consumers with the aim of selling products.

Place: the methods used by a firm to sell its products or services to consumers.

Activity

1. Choose a product offered by a small business in your area that you know well, such as your local newsagent, internet café or sports shop. With each of the 4Ps as a heading, describe the mix that is being used.

∞ links

Go to **www.astonmartin.com** to see how a marketing mix can give a clear message about a firm's products.

Is there a right image?

This question depends on who the business expects to be the type of person to buy its product or service. Most businesses can describe their **target market**. For example, the theme park Thorpe Park targets 14–25-year-old 'thrill seekers' from South East England, and sets its marketing mix to appeal mostly to people in this age range with a 'thrill-seeking' attitude. A small start-up business may well have a smaller target market geographically, or a cosmetic business may mainly target females, but whatever the business, the starting point of an effective marketing plan is a clear idea of what type of person they are trying to sell to.

With this in mind the firm can make its decisions on the marketing mix with the target market in mind, setting a mix that is most likely to lead to sales success.

Adjusting the mix with a limited budget

At the time of writing, the newspapers are full of news stories about firms closing because of a lack of customers. The UK economy is entering a period of recession. As a result, businesses are adjusting their marketing mix to suit the times. Marks & Spencer is offering 'three for the price of two'. Poundland and other stores are spending more money advertising their 'budget' stores to a wider range of consumers. Economic changes can force firms to change their marketing mix as their target market experiences different circumstances. Some marketing options might be too expensive for small firms with a very limited budget, but this does not mean they cannot do anything.

Example 1: Alex and his website design business might offer more interactive facilities on new websites for a lower price (see 'Meet the entrepreneurs' in the Unit 1 opener).

Example 2: Nilesh could offer a reduced price if customers agreed to have both the inside and the outside of their properties decorated (see 'Meet the entrepreneurs' in Unit 1 opener).

Other changes in the world can force firms to change their marketing mix, with increased environmental concerns forcing petrol companies such as Shell to base their advertising on their 'green' credentials, whilst McDonald's has been forced to offer healthier eating alternatives as a result of growing concerns over obesity.

Technological change can force firms to rethink which products they are selling, whilst laws might force some companies to change the way their products are promoted, with unhealthy food adverts now banned from children's television.

Example 3: A new takeaway pizza business might promote the fact that all of its ingredients are organic and that all the packaging is recyclable.

Activity

2   Using the same product that you chose for the last activity, describe the type of person you think the small business is trying to target, and briefly explain whether the 4Ps used appeal to this type of customer.

AQA   *Examiner's tip*

Stress the importance of a marketing mix that gives out the same image in your answer. Point out how important it is to make sure that all of the 4Ps are giving off the same message about the business and the product.

B   *Alex and Nilesh adjusted their working practices to attract new clients*

What goods or service should we try and sell? This decision more than any other will make or break a small business. The 'product decision' does not end here though. Even a small firm making just one product is likely to make a number of different versions, designed to appeal to different types of people. All businesses are likely to have a **product range**. Different types of people make up the target market for each product. Over time, some products will become out of date and will need to be updated or replaced by products that are technologically more advanced.

What products do small firms produce?

Let's look at our entrepreneurs again (see 'Meet the entrepreneurs' in the Unit 1 opener). In most start-up businesses, entrepreneurs will choose to supply a good service that:

They know quite a lot about

Alex is a computer expert and Ania is a knowledgeable gardener:

Alex

Ania

They are really interested in

Nilesh is very keen to help disadvantaged groups with his decorating skills.

Does not require a lot of money

Minseung could start a dog-sitting service with practically no money at all.

Nilesh

Minseung

Does not require a large building or expensive equipment

This applies to all four of our entrepreneurs.

Why small firms adapt their products

Just making one type of products or offering the same service to every customer is unusual. Many small firms try to adapt their goods and services to the special needs of customers. This approach is likely to:

- increase sales
- increase customer loyalty.

Here are some examples:

- Ania might start to offer a full garden-design service for customers who have moved to a new house.
- Alex might offer a regular update service for websites designed by his business that need to be updated frequently. For example, one of his customers sells stamps over the internet so his stock is constantly changing.
- A small beauty salon with a spare room might offer this to a hairdresser to style customers' hair.
- A Chinese restaurant located in an area where many Polish building workers are employed might offer special Polish menus at lunchtime. This is a form of **product differentiation**.

Why the product is important

Small firms produce goods or services that the owners know something about or that reflects the skills or interests they have. The original choice of product sometimes has to be adapted to meet the needs of different customers, in order to increase sales. Small businesses may also change their products to reflect competitors' product decisions and technological changes.

Activity

Use examples of **two** local small businesses that you are aware of. For each business suggest **one** way it could change the products it offers to meet different customer needs.

Did you know ??????

The product is the key decision taken by a small business – the other parts of the marketing mix must be based around the product decision.

Key terms

Product range: the collective term given to all the products made or sold by a business.

Product differentiation: attempting to make your products stand out from those of your rivals through advertising, design or different product features.

A *Companies often make different versions of their products to appeal to different parts of the market*

2.5 The marketing mix: price

Deciding how much to charge for a product or service is not a simple task. An entrepreneur running a start-up business may not have any experience in price setting. Several factors will affect the decision made by a small business, but perhaps the primary consideration will be the effect that price has on the demand for the product.

Price and demand

We often use the term **demand** as a quick way to express the total quantity of a product that consumers want to and can afford to buy. Thinking about demand in this way, it should be easy to understand how demand for a product changes if the price changes.

Activity

1. Assuming that you are typical of most people, fill in the second column in the table below:

Price of an average download of a music track	Number per month that you would buy
20p	
40p	
50p	
£1	

2. Now put your results on a graph with the y-axis labelled 'Number of downloads' and x-axis labelled 'Price'.

The graph you drew in the activity should show a line going downwards from left to right. This is typical of almost every good or service available – the lower the price, the more of it consumers will buy.

The message for an entrepreneur is clear – to sell more, charge less for the product you are selling **or** make your product so special that consumers will be prepared to pay more than competitors' products.

Why not decide on a really low price?

Selling a product at a very low price, compared to similar products, will lead to very high demand. However, every small business needs to make a profit eventually. Price level has a role to play in making sure the firm makes a profit.

A simple rule to remember is that the price the business decides to set must *at least* pay for the cost of making/buying in the good or providing the service. Failure to set a price that covers costs will lead to a loss.

A   *Do computer buyers want low prices or quality products?*

Key terms

Demand: the quantity that consumers are willing and able to buy at the current price level.

A balancing act

Deciding price is something of a balancing act between covering costs and keeping the price low to encourage people to buy.

Other factors that influence the pricing decision include:

- the prices charged by competitors – unless the entrepreneur's product is very different to that of rival firms, a similar price to these other businesses may have to be set

- larger businesses often have lower costs for making each product – smaller firms may have to accept a lower profit on each item or offer such a great level of personal customer service that buyers will pay more

- a start-up business may charge a very low price to attract new customers and then raise prices later – this is called 'penetration pricing' and is explained in more detail in Chapter 7.

Why pricing is important

Price will have a great impact on demand. The price level also makes a product seem to be good value or poor value.

Common sense is a vital part of any pricing decision, but these decisions will be improved by considering the factors covered within this section: demand, competitors and costs.

∞ links

Business Link is a government-funded organisation set up to offer advice to entrepreneurs. Go to its website, select 'Sales and marketing' and then click 'Pricing' and read the advice:
www.businesslink.gov.uk

AQA Examiner's tip

Always consider the wider effects of any price change. Student answers that advise a firm to cut its prices to sell more are in danger of ignoring the need to charge enough to still cover costs and hopefully make a profit.

B *Milk comes from the same place but can vary in price*

Activity

3 Check the prices of a 2½ litre bottle of milk from three different supermarkets.

a How much does the price vary?

b Why do you think some supermarkets are able to sell this and other products more cheaply?

2.6 The marketing mix: promotion

If nobody knows that a business exists it will not sell a thing. It is vital that new businesses find some way to spread their name and product details amongst potential customers. 'Promotion' is used to describe the methods used to communicate a message from the business to its customers or potential customers.

Know your budget limits

Almost every method of promoting a business will cost money, whether it is the cost of printing leaflets, or the cost of making and showing a television advert. Given unlimited money, any inexperienced manager could find a way to push a promotional message for a business. Marketing experts are those who manage to get the business's message across as cheaply as possible, but without making the business or its products seem cheap.

How much should you spend on promotion?

In the case of a small business this **marketing budget** could be very small, yet the owner will still have to do something to make the business known. Deciding which types of promotion to use, when, and how often to use them is a vital part of the role of a successful entrepreneur.

Activity

1 Look back at the entrepreneurs in the Unit 1 opener and think about how they might use their marketing budget.

What is your promotion trying to achieve?

- Awareness – a new business needs to make people aware that it exists and where it can be found.
- Information – promotion will be used to give consumers specific information about the products sold by the business.
- Brand and image building – promotion is a key part in any business's attempt to make itself and its products stand out from their competitors.

A Website promotion is increasingly used by businesses

Who do you promote to?

As has been explained, a well-prepared entrepreneur will have a fairly clear idea of the target market. It is this group of people that promotion will be aimed at. There is no point wasting money trying to sell a conservatory to someone who lives at the top of a block of flats. The more closely focused the promotion is on the target group of consumers the more cost-effective the promotion will be.

B *Promotion methods for small businesses*

Method of promotion	Advantages	Disadvantages
Advertising in local newspapers	■ Size can be adjusted to fit the budget. ■ Should allow a wide local audience to be reached.	■ May not be well targeted. ■ Paying for a large and well-designed advert can be expensive.
Free **publicity** (e.g. special shop-opening ceremony with a local celebrity)	■ If the news story is carried by the local paper and radio stations this is free! – the celebrity could cost a lot though.	■ The company does not control the content, so those reporting on the event may provide negative publicity (e.g. 'the shop was too small to hold all of the people who attended.').
Customer **word-of-mouth** recommendation	■ Free and trustworthy – most people believe their friends' advice.	■ Impossible to control – people may not talk about you, or they may spread a negative message about your business.
Direct mail or leaflets through letterboxes in local area	■ Once the letter/leaflet has been printed hand delivery is quite cheap – postal methods might not be, however.	■ Often seen as 'junk mail' and not read by consumers. ■ Leaflets and direct mail have quite a low success rate.
Promotion through **personal selling** of the product	■ Allows an individualised approach to selling to each customer.	■ May be seen as a nuisance, and the need to employ salespeople makes this method very expensive.
Website	■ Provides basic information to anyone searching for a product or business. ■ Can also be used for e-commerce when the product is sold online.	■ Needs regular maintenance to stay up to date and looking good. ■ Needs to be easily found through a reliable search engine.
Banners and **pop-ups** on other websites	■ Can target people by interest or hobby (e.g. a pet grooming business can use a banner advert on a dog-lovers' website).	■ May be ignored (banners), seen as a nuisance or even blocked (pop-ups).

Activity

2 A new computer set-up and repair service is planning to spend £500 promoting its business in the local area for the first six months. Use the following information to decide how it should spend its £500 and explain your choices.

■ Website: £40 per month to maintain.
■ Advert in *Yellow Pages*: £250 per year.
■ Advert in local paper: £50 per week.
■ Direct mailing 2,000 leaflets: £250 to print and distribute.
■ Publicity – hosting a special launch party to which local celebrities are invited: £500.
■ Advert on local radio station: £50 for two plays per day for a week.

AQA Examiner's tip

■ In your answers don't ignore the cost of promotion – it can be very expensive. Also remember that your first exam will be based on a small business, so cheap methods of promotion need to be used.
■ Do not fall into the trap of believing that all promotion is successful. Promotion may fail to boost sales if the wrong method or message is used.

2.7 The marketing mix: place

Getting the product to customers

This section will focus mainly on physical goods rather than services, such as dry cleaning and haircutting, which are usually provided directly to the consumer by the business. For physical goods, there are more options of getting the product to the consumer, which are known as **channels of distribution**. The main methods are shown in the Diagram **A**.

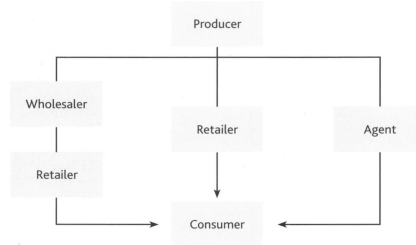

A *Traditional channels of distribution*

You can see that the product may pass through other businesses on its route from producer to consumer. These middlemen are known as 'intermediaries'. They each make their own profit as they buy the product at a lower price than they sell for.

In return for this profit, they will each offer their own benefits:

- Wholesalers – the major benefit of wholesalers is that they buy large quantities of a product from producers and break them down into more manageable batches for retailers or consumers.
- Retailers – the key function provided by retailers is to offer consumers a convenient and comfortable environment in which to buy products.

Online – the growth of e-commerce

An increasing number of small businesses are using the direct chain of distribution, delivering directly to customers. A few will use their own delivery vehicles, but most rely on distribution companies such as DHL, FedEx or Royal Mail.

Large companies selling via catalogues will use this chain too, but by far the most common use of the direct channel is **e-commerce**, where the consumer is buying from a business or auctions website.

Small firms can use the internet to reach a huge target market. A tiny start-up business can reach a global market by setting up a website.

Objectives

Understand the routes through which a small business can get its product to the final consumer.

Understand the growing importance of the internet in allowing sellers and buyers to meet.

Key terms

Channel of distribution: the method used to transfer goods or services from the producer to the final consumer.

e-commerce: transactions between people and business carried out entirely via the internet.

Research activity

1 Visit two or three small local retailers. Ask about how their products make their way from the producer to the shop itself. Try to find some who use wholesalers and some who buy direct from the producer.

Activity

1 Using Diagram **A**, select the most appropriate channel of distribution for each of the following types of product made by small businesses. Explain why you feel it is the most appropriate channel.

a Personalised key rings

b Specialist handmade chocolates

c Large wooden bedroom wardrobes

B Both small …

C … and large businesses use their websites to get service to their customers

Indeed, a small trader may be able to use a marketplace that already exists on the internet, such as eBay and Amazon.

Why place is important

■ The right channel will balance the need to cut costs (and therefore the final price) by using the most direct route possible with the need to get the product into as many different 'places' as possible so customers can access it when and where they want it.

■ Generally larger, bulkier items will use more direct channels, whilst smaller items, which may be impulse buys (e.g. soft drinks), will pass through several intermediaries to get the widest distribution possible.

Research activity

2 Look up the 'Market Place' on a website such as eBay, Amazon or Play.com and consider the advantages and disadvantages to small business.

Don't forget to think about how it allows them to reach international customers.

Finance and support for small businesses

Sources of finance

All businesses require finance at different stages of their life spans. This is simply a source of extra money for the business. Sources of finance are used for a whole range of reasons from getting the business through hard times, such as a recession, and good times when the business wants to expand.

A new business will need money to set up before they start trading. Cash is needed for things such as:

- equipment
- rent/mortgage of building
- advertising
- stock.

A   *Common sources of finance and how to obtain them*

Source of finance	Key term	Benefits	Disadvantages	Information and evidence needed to obtain it
Bank loan	Finance provided by the bank that will be paid back over a set period.	■ Large amounts can be borrowed that don't have to be paid back all at once.	■ Interest has to be paid, increasing costs. ■ Repayment terms must be met.	The bank is likely to want to see a cash flow forecast and possibly a business plan.
Loan from friends and family	Finance provided by friends or family where the interest rate and repayment periods are agreed with them.	■ They will be flexible about when you have to pay it back and might not charge interest.	■ They might not be able to afford to lend the entrepreneur very much.	Family and friends will depend on their trust in the business owner, but they may want to see details of the business plans too.
Overdrafts	A flexible arrangement that allows a business to spend more money than it has in its bank account, as and when it needs the finance.	■ Once it has been set up the business can use its overdraft arrangement as many times as it wants without having to ask the bank's permission every time.	■ Overdrafts normally have high interest rates attached to them and the bank can ask it to be paid back in full at any time.	Cash flow forecasts will need to be shown each time the overdraft arrangement is rearranged – perhaps every year.
Mortgage	Long-term loan for purchasing a building.	■ Often with a fixed rate of interest. ■ Repayments every month.	■ It may have a variable interest rate, which can become expensive if rates rise. ■ The lender may insist on 'security'.	The legal deeds of the property must be shown to the lender and may be kept by lender until mortgage is paid off.
Trade credit	Suppliers who allow debts for goods and services to be paid one or two months after delivery.	■ 'Free' finance is available for the period of the trade credit.	■ Discounts for immediate or quick payment may be lost.	References from the bank and possible other suppliers, and possibly a cash flow forecast.
Grants	Money given to a business by a government organisation or charity.	■ The money does not have to be paid back.	■ Many businesses do not qualify for them.	Many forms have to be filled out to prove the business is eligible for the grant.

When to use different sources

Different sources of finance are more appropriate for different situations. Before deciding which source of finance is best for them, a business should look to see if the need for finance is a short- or long-term one. If a business has a short-term finance problem then it should use a short-term solution, such as an overdraft or trade credit.

However, if the business needs a large amount of finance to pay back over a long period of time it should use a loan or a mortgage.

Financial support and advice

New businesses are not alone when it comes to choosing their source of finance. They can get expert help and advice. This advice can come from many different sources, but the most frequently used are:

B *Banks offer finance to start-up a business*

- High street banks – they all offer a business banking service and free advice to new business owners. For example, Barclays offers entrepreneurs free consultations with an accountant, lawyer and marketing expert.

- Government organisations such as the Regional Development Agencies (RDA) – these are committed to improving economic conditions in all regions of the UK. They have helped 56,000 new businesses since 2002. RDA experts will help entrepreneurs with applying for grants and making contacts with other businesses.

- Charitable organisations such as The Prince's Trust – this focuses on helping 18–30-year-old unemployed people set up their own businesses. Advice from business experts is provided as well as grants, low interest rate loans and long-term contact with an experienced business manager or mentor.

Activities

1 Investigate the following sources of finance for a new business that plans to restore buildings. Explain the benefits and drawbacks for each business.

a Business grants

b Bank loans

c Overdraft.

2 In groups, come up with a business idea and then decide:

a approximately how much finance you think will be needed

b what sources of finance you will need

c what information you will need to provide to obtain the finance.

3 Look on the two links provided and investigate the support and advice they can give to the new business you thought of above.

AQA Examiner's tip

Before choosing what source of finance a business should consider, you need to think about what the money is for, how much is needed and how quickly it will have to be paid back.

⊂⊃links

Find out more at:

www.princes-trust.org.uk

www.englandsrdas.com

3.2 | Financial terms and basic financial calculations

Running a small business can be stressful and can cause the owners to have a lot of sleepless nights. Two big worries for entrepreneurs are:

- Am I making a **profit** or a **loss**? Owners worry about profit because if the business makes a profit then it should improve their lifestyle, but if it makes a loss the business may eventually close and the owners' possessions might have to be sold to pay off the business debts.
- Do I have enough cash to pay for my expenses? Owners worry about cash as this is used to pay for the day-to-day running **costs** of the business. Without cash the business will not be able to pay workers, suppliers or any other bills and it will fail.

Cash flow and the difference between this and profit is covered in the next section.

Calculating revenue

To work out **revenue**, multiply the amount of products sold, for example, 10,000 hotdogs a year, by the selling price, £2.50 a hotdog.

Revenue = number sold × selling price

The revenue for the hotdogs is shown below:

£25,000 = 10,000 × £2.50

So, to increase revenue the hotdog stand owner has two choices:

- Increase the selling price and hope sales don't go down.
- Increase the amount sold, possibly through promotion such as advertising, which of course will increase costs too.

Calculating costs

This is as obvious as it seems. Any business will have things they have to spend money on, such as rent, wages, and the materials to make products. When all these costs are added together they are called 'total costs'. For example our hotdog stand might have the following costs each year:

A

Rent of site	£2,000
Wages	£12,000
Stock	£6,000
Equipment	£500
Fuel	£1,000
Total costs	**£21,500**

Now you have seen the different parts of the profit calculation you can put it all together and work out profit for yourself. Practise this by completing Activity 1 opposite.

Calculating profit (or loss)

To calculate profit you need two figures: revenue and total costs.

Profit (or loss) = revenue – costs

Look at these two examples to see how it works.

Vivien's nail bar has sales revenue of £40,000 for the year and total costs of £33,000. We can see she makes a profit of £7,000.

Profit (or loss) = revenue – costs

£40,000 – £33,000 = £7,000 (profit)

Jonell's sales revenue from his pet shop was £35,000 last year, but his costs were £39,000. We can see he makes a loss of £4,000.

Profit (or loss) = revenue – costs

£35,000 – £39,000 = –£4,000 (loss)

B   Hotgod stand

Activity

2   Use the profit and loss formula (Profit (or loss) = revenue – costs) to calculate the profit for these businesses. (Hint: You will need to use the revenue sum shown earlier.)

Business name	Selling price	Units sold per year	Revenue	Total costs	Profit
Haroons Taylor	£500 per suit	200 suits a year		£70,000	
Alex's Barbers	£10 a haircut	3,000 haircuts a year		£19,000	
Shamara's florist	£15 on average a bunch of flowers	2,500 bunches a year		£40,000	

3.3 Cash flow and survival

Difference between cash and profit

Cash and profit are not necessarily the same. This is very important in business. It means that:

- A profitable business could run out of cash – just because a company has made a profit does not mean it will have large amounts of **cash** sitting around. The profits may have been reinvested into new stock, using up spare cash, or the profit might have been created by selling on credit to customers. This means that although on paper lots of revenue and profit is going to be made from these credit sales, until the customer pays at the end of the credit period the company has little cash.
- A business making a loss could have plenty of cash – a retail business making a large monthly loss might sell its delivery van for cash. It therefore has money in the bank from the sale of the van, but the monthly costs of the shop are still greater than monthly revenue.

Why cash is important

If a business is to survive, cash is absolutely vital. Trying to run a business without enough cash is like trying to drive a car without enough fuel. The car might be in perfect condition, but without fuel the car simply does not work. If a business does not have cash it can not buy stock to sell, pay workers to run the business or even rent a property to operate from.

Cash is received mainly from:

- finance put into the business, such as the owner's savings or a loan
- sales paid for in cash
- payments from customers who have been given extra time to pay rather than paying straight away (credit sales).

Cash flow forecasts

Cash is so important to a business most sensible owners **forecast** the amount they will be likely to receive and spend. The way they forecast cash is by producing a **cash flow forecast**. This is a table that shows predicted future cash in and out of the business and very importantly the closing balance.

To be able to fully understand one and comment on it you need to identify all of the different parts that make up a cash flow forecast. Table **A** shows a cash flow forecast with each section explained.

Receipts/income is the money the business is paid in the month. It may be from cash sales or credit sales. To calculate it you just add together all the money the company receives that month.

Payments/expenditure is anything that the business spends that month, such as the rent. To calculate it you just add together all the money the company spends that month.

A A cash flow forecast

	Jan (£)	Feb (£)
Receipt (cash in)	10,000	12,000
Payments (cash out)	12,000	11,000
Net cash flow	(2,000)	1,000
Opening balance	3,000	1,000
Closing balance	1,000	2,000

Net cash flow is the difference between the receipts and payments.

Net cash flow = receipts – payments

Opening balance is the money the business has at the start of the month. It is the closing balance from the previous month.

Closing balance is the money the company has at the end of the month.

Closing balance = net cash flow + opening balance

Table **B** shows a further example of a simple cash flow statement, for Nana's Sports Shop. As we can see from the closing balance on the cash flow forecast, it predicts that there will be big problems in January and February, but that there should be a lot of spare cash available in June. Nana can now use this to plan for the future finance needs of the business.

B Cash flow forecast for Nana's Sports Shop

	Jan (£)	Feb (£)	Mar (£)	Apr (£)	May (£)	Jun (£)
Receipt (cash in)	5,000	7,500	9,000	8,000	8,500	8,400
Payments (cash out)	15,000	3,250	4,500	4,000	4,250	4,200
Net cash flow	–10,000	4,250	4,500	4,000	4,250	4,200
Opening balance	1,000	–9,000	–4,750	–250	3,750	8,000
Closing balance	–9,000	–4,750	–250	3,750	8,000	12,200

■ Why a cash flow forecast is important

Forecasting cash flow in advance gives the business owner several benefits:

- It allows the owner to check they will have enough cash available over the next few months to keep the business going. If they don't, they can try and get a source of finance to help, such as arranging an overdraft.
- It allows the owner to try to reduce future outflows of cash so that the business can avoid running out of cash.
- It may help persuade the bank to lend the business money or give it an overdraft. This is because the owner can predict that it has enough spare cash each month to make repayments.
- The forecasted numbers can be used as targets for the owner to aim at and check if the business is meeting these targets.

3.4 Using cash flow forecasts

In the previous two sections we looked at how to calculate a company's profit or loss and what a cash flow forecast looks like. It is important now to look at cash flow forecasts in a little more depth. At the end of this section you will be able to interpret exactly what they show and comment on them, as you may be asked to do this in your exam.

■ Interpreting a cash flow forecast

When looking at a cash flow forecast there are certain key things you should look out for:

- Cash in/receipts – you would hope to see this figure increasing over time as the business gets more customers. If the receipts are getting smaller this is worrying as it probably means sales are falling.
- Cash out/payments – apart from setting up the business and the occasional one-off extra cost, the payments should increase at almost the same rate as the receipts as the more you sell, the more you will have to buy. It would be worrying if payments kept going up but receipts were going down.
- Closing balance – what is left at the end of each time period is probably the easiest and biggest area to comment on. In general, you would want it to be improving over time as the business grows and receipts increase. However, it is common for it to be a negative number at the start of a new business as a lot of payments may have been made to set up the business.

Activities

1 Look at the cash flow statement below and comment on the following areas, pointing out **one** good and **one** bad thing about each:

a Receipts
b Payments
c Closing balance.

A

	Jan (£)	Feb (£)	Apr (£)	May (£)	June (£)	July (£)
Receipt (cash in)	4,000	5,000	6,500	6,000	5,500	4,500
Payments (cash out)	10,000	2,500	3,250	3,000	2,750	2,250
Net cash flow	6,000	2,500	3,250	3,000	2,750	2,250
Opening balance	3,000	–3,000	–500	2,750	5,750	8,500
Closing balance	–3,000	–500	2,750	5,750	8,500	10,750

2 Look at the months of January and February in the cash flow forecast. What cash flow solutions would you suggest the business uses. Explain your choice and make sure you read the Examiner's tip before answering.

Identifying solutions to cash flow problems

Once you have looked at a cash flow forecast it may become apparent that the business is going to have problems with its cash flow in certain months. However, this is not a disaster as there are several possible solutions for cash flow problems.

- Make payments to your supplier at a later date, when you think you will have more spare cash. However, a supplier may not be keen to do this as it may be detrimental to their cash flow.

- Encourage receipts to be paid earlier. This simply means trying to persuade your customers to pay soon if they have bought on credit. However, to do this you may have to offer them a discount deal, which could mean you lose out on profit in the long run.

- Use a source of finance such as a loan, if a large amount is needed and you want time to pay it back, or an overdraft, if the business needs extra money for the short term, for example, to stock up on toys in a toyshop before Christmas.

- Cut payments by finding ways of reducing costs, such as making a worker unemployed. However, this will obviously upset the other workers and may mean more work for the owner.

B *Cash flow problems hit established companies too*

The solution to cash flow problems depends on the size of the problem and whether it is caused by increasing payments or falling receipts.

Activities

3 Think of two businesses that might offer their customers credit.

4 Explain what cash flow problems offering credit might cause these businesses.

5 Look at the cash flow forecast in Activity 1 and suggest solutions to the cash flow problems.

6 Some people might suggest a January sale would improve a shop's cash flow position. Why might a sale reduce profit?

AQA Examiner's tip

Remember that when suggesting solutions to cash flow problems there will be disadvantages as well, such as suggesting advertising to increase sales. This will cost money and worsen the cash flow in the short term.

Case study

Nana's sport shop has a problem. To attract more customers, it offered them 3 months' credit on any purchases over £100. This looked like a great idea to start with, as lots of new customers came to the shop to take advantage of the offer. However, after two months of offering the credit, Nana had used up all his spare cash buying stock to meet the new demand so couldn't afford to buy any more or pay other bills. To make matters worse, lots of his customers still don't have to pay what they owe for another month.

Suggest solutions to help Nana with his cash flow problems. You should explain your answers.

4.1   People in business: recruiting

Once an entrepreneur has decided that they need to hire some employees, there are certain factors they should consider before going ahead so that they recruit the best possible employees who will help earn profits for the business.

When to recruit workers

For a small business, such as those run by our entrepreneurs, the need to **recruit** new staff is most likely in particular circumstances:

- When the business expands, as it has more customers than can be served by the business owner. Nilesh, the entrepreneur who set up his own decorating business, might be turning away new customers because he is always so busy.
- When an existing worker leaves or is dismissed and needs to be replaced. Alex, the website designer, employed a student from college for a trial period, but his work was very slow, so Alex hopes to recruit a new member of staff.

New staff can be employed on a **part-time** or **full-time** basis.

Full time or part time?

When a business owner decides they need some help, the first question to answer is: 'Should a full-time or part-time employee be recruited?'

A   *Advantages of recruiting full-time and part-time workers*

Full-time workers	Part-time workers
Fewer staff in total will be needed as they work more hours per week.	The number of customers may not justify a full-time worker, so a part-time worker saves on wages.
Lower recruitment and training costs.	Two workers may be more flexible than one full-time worker (e.g. able to cover for absence).
Easier to manage and control fewer staff.	Part-time workers can be asked to work just at busy times of the day or week. This could lead to better customer service and a competitive advantage.
Workers may feel more secure and motivated having a full-time job and earning more money than if they worked part time.	Some workers may prefer part-time employment, for example, if they have children to look after.
If a worker has two separate part-time jobs they may have divided loyalties – this should not be a problem with full-time workers.	

B   *An advert for a part-time job in a shop window*

◼ Recruitment methods

Once the business owner has decided to recruit a member of staff, they should follow these simple stages.

⊂⊃ links

Job descriptions and specifications are covered in more detail in Chapter 9.

Case study

Asif needs help

Asif set up his satellite navigation fitting business six months ago. He buys 'satnav' kits cheaply from the internet and fits them to customers cars. He works 12 hours a day but still finds little time to do the accounts of the business, greet new customers or redesign the website of the business. Some customers have gone to competing firms because of the long wait for service. He decides to recruit someone to help him but he really does not know how to go about it. He has never employed anyone other than himself!

Activities

1 Explain the benefits to Asif's business if he employed someone to help him.

2 How would you advise Asif to advertise this vacancy? Explain your answer.

3 Would you advise Asif to employ one worker for 36 hours per week or two workers for 18 hours per week each? Explain your answer.

Step 1: job description

They need to decide what kind of work they want the employee to do.

Step 2: person specification

They need to decide what kind of person they are looking for.

Step 3: advertise the job vacancy

Where the business advertises will depend on what type of worker it is after, whether to use **internal** or **external recruitment** and how much they want to pay. If you are after an unskilled local worker, there is no point paying lots of money to advertise in a national newspaper; a better place may be the local jobcentre. Some other places to advertise include local newspapers, your own business's window, staff notice board or by word of mouth.

The job advert needs to include:

- ▪ job title
- ▪ what the job involves
- ▪ pay
- ▪ hours
- ▪ where the job is
- ▪ company name
- ▪ how to apply.

C *Newspapers are often used by employers to advertise vacancies*

Activity

4 Draw up a suitable newspaper advertisement for a new Business Studies teacher in your school.

Alex decided to advertise the vacancy in his website design business on the internet. He thinks that the type of person he is looking for is most likely to use computers and not newspapers to look for jobs.

An alternative to advertising, which can be expensive for a small business, even in a local newspaper, is personal recommendation. This is when one or more people who might be suitable for the job vacancy are recommended to the business owner by:

- other employees
- family or friends of the business owner
- business colleagues.

Very often these personal contacts, if they are from people who can be trusted, are an effective method of recruitment as the person being recommended, their loyalty, skills and honesty, should be well known to the person who recommends them.

Step 4: shortlist candidates

After advertising or receiving personal recommendations, the owner then chooses the best few people to interview or give a trial to. This is called 'shortlisting'. This shortlisting could be decided by:

- the strength of the personal recommendations
- the details given on the application form
- past experience, skills and qualifications of the applicants – all of these would have been detailed on each applicant's curriculum vitae (CV), which is a summary of an applicant's education and jobs to date.

Step 5: interviews

This is a very common way of selecting workers. It is only natural that the business owner would want to meet potential workers and ask them some key questions. Some of the most common job interview questions include:

- Why do you want to work for this business?
- What do you think you can offer this business?
- What do you think are your greatest strengths and weaknesses?
- When would you be able to start work, if you were appointed?

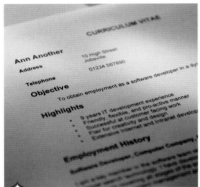

D A curriculum vitae helps to secure an interview

E Interviewing is an integral part in employing new staff

Asif was just as nervous as the three people he had asked for interview. He had decided to employ someone to help him fit 'satnav' kits so that his business could continue to expand. He wanted them to deal directly with customers. They had to know a lot about car electrics and the fitting of equipment. They would also be required to fill out paperwork for each job and to drive customers' cars.

Activities

5 Write out **three** questions that you think Asif should ask each applicant (apart from those in the list above).

6 Explain briefly why you think each question is important.

After the interviews or trial, the best person should be offered the job. However, the business owner needs to know all of the legal limits on this very important decision. See pages 70–1 for more on this.

When a job vacancy arises in a business, especially a post that carries some responsibility, it could be offered either to a worker who is currently employed by the firm or it could be advertised externally. There are important benefits of both types of recruitment.

F *Advantages of internal and external recruitment*

Internal recruitment	External recruitment
The business owner will already know the worker's strengths, skills and weaknesses.	New ideas and skills ('fresh blood') may be brought into the business, which internal applicants for the vacant post might not have.
Little additional training will be required unless the job vacancy is for a different position.	The selection process will have many more applicants than when using internal recruitment, so the standard of applicant could be high.
It is cheaper than external recruitment as no external advertising or lengthy selection process will be needed.	It does not create another vacancy in the business, which then has to be filled.
Employees in the business will feel that there is a chance to develop their career and this could make staff more loyal.	Internal promotion can cause jealousy amongst other current workers who may have wanted the job but were not offered it.

Olly owns a small female-only hairdressers in Cambridge. During the past year his business has gained an excellent reputation as the most fashionable in the area and demand has gone up and up. To take advantage of this popularity Olly wants to open a male hair salon next door, but would need to recruit a manager, a hairdresser and a trainee for it.

Activities

7 For each job explain whether Olly should use personal recommendation instead of advertising. Justify your answer.

8 Assume that Olly is not happy with the people who have been recommended to him. Where would you recommend he advertises for each job? Justify your answer.

9 What advantages might Olly gain from employing part-time rather than full-time workers?

G *Olly wishes to expand his salon*

Employees rarely work for nothing! Workers will expect financial rewards in the form of pay, and many also expect other additional benefits as well. Deciding how much to pay workers and any additional benefits can have a significant impact on worker motivation and loyalty.

Deciding how much to pay employees

Either when recruiting staff or when trying to keep them motivated and keen to stay with the business, important decisions must be made by the business owner. These include:

- how much to pay the worker or applicant for a job
- what other benefits (monetary and non-monetary) should be offered.

The three most important factors that influence the pay decision are:

Skills needed by the job

Normally, the more skills and qualifications needed for a job the better the pay. For example, if the job requires no special or rare skills, like a cleaner, then the pay will often be low, as anybody could do it. However, if the job needs a highly skilled and qualified worker, like a doctor, then the salary is likely to be high. Ania, the gardening entrepreneur, needed to recruit a worker who was skilled at using diggers and other landscaping equipment. She knew she would have to pay higher wages than if she employed someone without this skill.

Experience of the worker

A worker who has many years of experience will expect to be paid more than an inexperienced person. This is because their experience should mean they have dealt with many different situations so can offer better advice to the business and may need less training, which will save the business money.

How much other similar local firms are paying

Workers tend to prefer to work for firms that pay the highest wages, so even small businesses may have to consider the pay levels of other local firms when setting pay levels for their workers.

> **Objectives**
>
> Understand the factors that influence the level of wages/salaries paid to workers.
>
> Understand the use of other monetary benefits.
>
> Understand the use of non-monetary benefits.

> **Did you know ??????**
>
> You can find out what workers earn in your local area by reading the local paper to compare pay rates. How can differences in rates be explained?

Case study

Jim's Garage

Jim's Garage employs four workers. One is in charge of the petrol pumps and the petrol office. One is a skilled mechanic with a qualification from Volkswagen that took three years of apprenticeship to gain. Two others are general helpers in both the workshop and the petrol office. All four workers think that the pay levels in Jim's garage are too low.

- Advise Jim what factors he should consider in deciding how much to pay each worker.

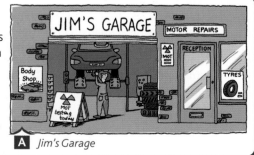

A Jim's Garage

■ Attracting and keeping the best employees

When recruiting, a business is competing with many other companies for the best workers. To ensure they get the best, a business will not only have to pay well, but may need to offer other benefits.

Other monetary benefits

These are other ways that the employee will get money while doing the job, other than receiving the basic **wage** or **salary**, such as bonuses for reaching targets. For example, an employee in a call centre may get a bonus for reaching a target number of calls in a day. Another monetary benefit is if the company agrees to pay money into the employees' **pension**. This will be paid out on retirement. Generous pension schemes are becoming increasingly rare as they are very expensive, especially for small firms, but they do have a significant effect on worker loyalty towards a business.

Non-monetary rewards

These are extra items that the employee is given while they work at the company, such as a company car, private health scheme or free mobile phone. These **non-monetary rewards** are normally called **fringe benefits**. Most small firms will offer a staff discount off the goods or services they provide. Entrepreneurs need to be careful though, as fringe benefits can add a great amount to the cost of employing workers in a small business, but they can make a business very popular to work for.

Nilesh offered the free use of his business estate car to the new employee when she moved flat – she was delighted with this generous thought.

Activities

Read the information in Table **B** on the two applicants for the job of a new chef at a small local Italian restaurant. Assume you are the restaurant owner.

1 Which applicant would you recruit and why?

2 The average pay for a chef in the area is £16,000–£29,000. What level of pay would you offer the successful applicant? Explain your answer.

3 Would you offer any other rewards or fringe benefits? Explain your answer.

B

	Applicant A	Applicant B
Name	Lucy Tse	Alex Phillips
Qualifications	A* in GCSE food technology	C grade in GCSE food technology
	BTEC National diploma in food hygiene	BTEC National diploma in catering
Experience	1 year as a trainee chef at Frankie and Benny's Italian restaurant	2 years as a trainee at a local Italian restaurant in Milan
	1 year as a chef at Pizza Express	5 years as head chef at three different Italian restaurants in London
Skills and qualities	Good team worker	Good communicator
	Pastry specialist	Pasta-making specialist
Current salary and benefits	£12,000 salary plus share of tips	£290 per week plus bonuses for good attendance
	Company pension scheme	Private health insurance scheme

4.3 Motivating staff

What is motivation?

Motivation is the desire to do something. People can be motivated by many things, such as fear, love and money. In simple terms, the more motivated we are the harder we will work.

Why is motivation important?

Motivated staff can be the difference between a small business succeeding or failing. This is because motivated employees work harder, make fewer mistakes and are pleasant and helpful to customers. These advantages can result in the business gaining a good reputation. They are basically good value for money and bring in more customers and therefore profits.

Unmotivated employees are the opposite. They don't care about their job, so make mistakes that cost money, can be lazy, do little work for what they are paid, and can be rude to customers, gaining the business a bad reputation. No small business can afford these extra costs and a bad reputation, so motivated employees are essential.

Motivating staff in a small business

If you were to ask the people in your class what motivates them, they are likely to say money. They are right to some extent, as employees will often be more motivated by monetary rewards. However, in reality, employees are not just motivated by money but also by non-financial factors.

A *Motivating staff can help them to work harder*

Monetary techniques

To motivate its workers a small business may offer money as an incentive, such as bonuses for reaching targets or possibly **commission** on the items they sell. These techniques motivate staff, as they obviously want the money. However, they can end up costing a small business a lot of money. Another drawback is that employees may also become demotivated if they don't reach their targets and get the extra money.

Non-monetary techniques

Motivation can come from many other factors too. You will have experienced these factors in different lessons around your school. In some lessons you may be very motivated as you find the work interesting, and feel the teacher trusts you and cares about your education. However, in others you may be bored and not like how the teacher makes you work, so are demotivated and do less work. In the same way, similar factors can motivate or demotivate employees. Small businesses can use a number of non-monetary techniques to try and make staff interested in their jobs and keen to do well.

Objectives

Understand the benefits to business of motivated staff.

Understand the main methods of motivation used by small businesses.

Key terms

Commission: when the employee gets a percentage of the amount they sell. For example, estate agents may get 1 per cent of the value of every house they sell.

Training programmes

If workers are offered the chance to gain further skills, this benefits both the business and the worker. The person will feel important and special as they have been singled out for special training. In addition, many studies within business organisations have shown that training and the sense of achievement it brings can be very motivating and rewarding. In a small business this training might allow a worker to take over the running of one section or department, which will provide job satisfaction.

Offering responsibility

If workers are shown trust by being given responsibility over part of the business, the employees' work life will become more interesting and they will feel a sense of achievement, and therefore motivated. In a small business this sense of responsibility could be increased when a worker is trusted with looking after the business in the absence of the owner. Once Jo had proved herself, Alex gave her full responsibility for dealing with a client who wanted a special animated website – this was a particular area of interest for Jo.

B *Some companies offer apprenticeships or training programmes*

Case study

Sasha's reward

Sasha was determined to ask her employer for a pay rise. She had found out that another local firm of beauticians were paying their staff at least £2 an hour more than she was receiving.

'I cannot afford to pay you this much' explained Joanna, the owner of the beauty salon where Sasha worked. 'I really want to keep you as you are great with customers and we get on so well. Suppose I pay you £1 an hour more but give you the responsibility of running the shop on Saturday mornings. I will also pay for the advanced nail care training course that you told me about.'

Sasha agreed quickly to these rewards for her hard work.

Activity

1   Explain why Sasha seemed willing to work for Joanna for lower wages than she could have earned with another employer.

> **Did you know** ??????
>
> Small firms do not motivate staff by just paying more – training courses can be very rewarding too.

Activities

2   Ask five different members of your class what motivates them to work hard.

3   Discuss in small groups why people are motivated differently.

4   Explain why motivated employees are important to a small business.

5   Explain which motivational methods you would use to motivate the following types of employees:

a   teacher

b   worker in a fast-food restaurant

c   apprentice plumber

d   architect.

Occasionally some companies treat workers poorly and act unfairly towards them. This is usually because the business owner wants to reduce costs or because they think the workers can be easily replaced. Poor treatment of workers has led to lots of legislation (laws) to try and protect workers. Any small business that has employees or is looking to recruit some, needs to be aware of this legislation and how it will affect them. In the rest of this chapter we will cover the main legislation small businesses need to be aware of.

Equal Pay Act 1970

This piece of legislation means that employers must pay both men and women equal rates for the same jobs. Basically, you cannot pay somebody more or less than another worker just because of what sex they are. If a newsagents paid delivery boys £6 a round but girls only £5 a round, the owner would be breaking the Equal Pay Law.

Minimum Wage Act 1998

This sets out the minimum wage per hour a business is allowed to pay its workers. The minimum depends on age and an employer cannot pay less per hour, even if the worker was willing to work for a lower wage. Table **A** shows the minimum wage rates at the time of writing. You can check to see if it has changed using the website in the Link box. If an electrician operating as a sole trader had a 17-year-old trainee apprentice then he must pay the trainee at least £3.53 per hour (2008 rates). If the electrician refused to increase this rate on the apprentice's 18th birthday, he would be breaking the Minimum Wage Law.

Discrimination legislation

Discrimination legislation makes it illegal to discriminate against any person in the workplace on grounds of sex, age, race or disability. Examples are the Race Discrimination Act of 1976 and the Disability Discrimination Act of 1995. Therefore, when a business is deciding who to employ, train or promote they are not allowed to base their decision on sex, race, age or disability. If they do they are discriminating. If a newly opened florist shop advertised a vacancy for a shop assistant and the best qualified and experienced applicant was registered disabled, it would be breaking the Disability Discrimination Law not to employ this person.

Employment rights

All businesses must make sure they have the right insurance against injuries to employees. Also, employees have the right to several other things, such as sick pay, maternity or paternity leave, holidays and so on. So when a business draws up a contract of employment for the employee all these need to be covered.

Objectives

Understand how equal pay and minimum wage laws affect businesses.

Understand the laws against discrimination at work and during recruitment.

Understand employment rights of workers.

Understand health and safety laws.

∞ links

Find out the current minimum wage rates at: www.berr.gov.uk (search for 'minimum wage rate').

A *Minimum wage rates*

Age	Minimum wage per hour (December 2008)
16–17	£3.53
18–21	£4.77
22+	£5.73

Activity

1. Using the website in the Link box, find out the current minimum wage for all three age groups.

Health and Safety Acts

There are several of these laws and they generally state that employees have the right to work in a safe and healthy environment. However, this legislation also states that employees have a responsibility for their own health and safety, so must make sure they are acting in a safe way and don't put others at risk.

B *Guidelines for employing a new worker*

Do	Don't
Advertise in a way that encourages applicants from all sectors of society.	Include in the advertisements phrases such as: ■ Only women need apply. ■ No applications from disabled people will be considered. ■ Only black people will be considered.
Pay at least the minimum wage for different age groups.	Pay less than the minimum wage.
Offer a written contract of employment stating the worker's rights and responsibilities.	Insist they work with dangerous machines with no training or protection.
Select the best person for the job and keep evidence that the selection was not biased and did not discriminate in any way.	Pay women less than men, or vice versa.
Offer training to all new staff, especially when equipment or vehicles are involved.	Employ workers below the legal age for that particular job.

C *It is illegal to employ workers to operate this machinery without training and safety clothing*

AQA **Examiner's tip**

You will not be required to name and quote specific laws in the examination, such as the Equal Pay Act of 1970. You will just have to understand them and be able to explain their effect on a small business.

If a small business ignores the legislation mentioned in this chapter and ends up breaking the law there can very serious consequences. The business may be taken to court by an employee and possibly fined, closed down and, in the worst cases, the owner could be sent to jail.

Employee wins age discrimination case

A 20-year-old woman sacked by a private members club for being 'too young' has won an important age discrimination case. Megan Thomas worked as a membership secretary at the Eight Members Club in London. She thought she had been unfairly dismissed by managers after being told she was 'not old enough to deal with its members'.

A ruling by a London Employment Tribunal, thought to be the first about discrimination against younger people, ruled that Thomas was unfairly dismissed and discriminated against because of her age. After the ruling Thomas said: 'I was told I was too young and if they had met me a few years later there may not have been a problem.'

www.caterersearch.com, 15 November 2007

Activity

2 Having read the case study, contemplate the following questions:

a Do you agree with the decision?

b How much compensation do you think Megan Thomas should be paid? Why?

c Do you think that workers should be protected from unfair treatment by employers? Explain your answer.

Case study

5.1 Production methods

Production means using resources of land, labour and capital to make goods and services. There are several methods of production, but the two that are most commonly used by new and small businesses are job production and batch production.

■ Job production

Common examples of businesses that use **job production** include architects who design different houses for different customers, tailors and dressmakers who make individual suits and dresses to satisfy each customer's demands, and wedding-cake bakers. This method of production is easier and cheaper to set up than other methods, which is why it is suitable for new and small businesses.

Our entrepreneur Alex (see 'Meet the entrepreneurs' in the Unit 1 opener) will obviously be using job production because all of his customers require slightly different websites.

Objectives

Understand the main differences between job production and batch production.

Key terms

Job production: making one-off, specialised products for each customer.

Batch production: groups of identical items that pass through different stages of the production process at the same time.

A *Main features, advantages and disadvantages of job production*

Main features	Advantages	Disadvantages
Each product or service provided is aiming to satisfy the particular needs of one customer.	One-off products or services allow customers' special requirements to be met.	Production costs can be high. It is often a slow process as the business must plan and design each project individually.
It is a flexible production process – no two products or services need to be the same.	High prices can often be charged as customers may be prepared to pay extra for specially designed products.	Labour costs can be high as skilled workers are usually needed.

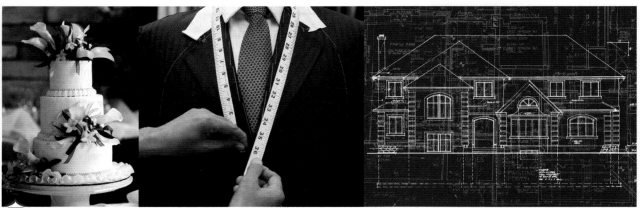

B *These products and services are often produced using job production*

■ Batch production

Common examples of **batch production** are paint manufacture, school uniforms, soft drinks and food in some takeaway restaurants. Try to imagine the cost and time involved in making each of these products with job production. How much would a can of cola cost you if it had been made as a one-off item especially for you?

Manufacturers that sell large quantities of products that are all exactly the same will often use batch production. It may be suitable for some small and newly formed businesses too. A new takeaway restaurant that plans to sell five main dishes would not make each customer's order on a job production basis. Large quantities of each dish could be made in advance and then reheated for each customer.

C *Main features, advantages and disadvantages of batch production*

Features	Advantages	Disadvantages
Groups of identical products can be made at the same time.	The cost of each unit produced is likely to be lower than job production as it is more efficient to make a lot of similar items.	There is less scope for customising products – consumers must be prepared to buy similar goods.
Different designs and styles can be made in different batches.	Different consumer tastes can be supplied by producing different products in different batches.	It can take a long time to switch from making a batch of one product to a batch of a different type of product.
To be profitable there must be demand for the same style, design or flavour of product.		Stocks of finished goods from each batch may take some time to sell.

D *Mass-market products such as cupcakes are often made using batch production*

Sarah specialises in pottery. She makes highly decorated plates. People buy these as presents after they have been decorated with names, places and events of the customer's choice. Each plate is different, but they are not cheap. Small plates cost £25 each and larger ones £35. An expert has forecast that one day Sarah's plates will become collector's items.

Case study

Activities

1 Which method of production does Sarah use?

2 Is this the best method of production for these products? Explain your answer.

James and Shivani have both just completed a bakery and cake-making course at college. They plan to bake rolls and speciality cakes to earn enough money to set up their own bakery shop. The bread rolls have been ordered by the canteen manager of their old school. The cakes would be made and decorated for birthdays and other celebrations.

Case study

Activity

3 Which methods of production would be most suitable for each product? Explain your answer.

Table **A** shows the production levels and costs of two small businesses that make wooden kitchen cupboards.

It is clear that Business A is more efficient – it has twice the number of workers of Business B, but produces four times as much. Each of its workers produces twice as many kitchen cupboards each year as a worker in Business B. As long as the cupboards made in both factories are of the same quality, Business A is more productively efficient.

So, what is the advantage of being **operationally efficient**? Compare the labour cost per cupboard figures. As each worker produces more cupboards, and is paid the same wage, the **unit cost** of labour is half that of Business B.

A *Can bespoke products be operationally efficient?*

Objectives

Understand what operational efficiency means.

Understand why operational efficiency can make a business more competitive.

B *Different levels of operational efficiency*

	Output level per year (units)	Total workers employed	Output per worker per year	Labour cost per worker per year	Labour cost per unit = labour cost/ output per worker
Business A	5,000	10	500	£10,000	£20
Business B	1,250	5	250	£10,000	£40

Advantages of being operationally efficient

This could give a big competitive advantage to Business A. It will be able to charge customers lower prices and still make a similar profit on each cupboard as Business B.

- If Business A lowered its prices it may even force Business B to make a loss if it reduced its prices too. This could eventually drive Business B out of business altogether.
- If our entrepreneur Nilesh (see 'Meet the entrepreneurs' in the Unit opener) expands his business to employ other decorators, he will want them to work as efficiently as possible and achieve a high-quality service to be as competitive as possible.

Key terms

Operational efficiency: producing goods and services to an acceptable standard with as few resources as possible to keep costs per unit low.

Unit costs: the average cost of making each unit.

How can one firm be more operationally efficient than another?

- More efficient machinery – perhaps using the latest advanced technology (see case study below). But, this machinery is often expensive.

- More highly motivated workers who want to work quickly and well. How can workers be motivated to work hard?

- Minimum wastage, meaning that virtually everything that is produced can be sold. This means making sure everything that is produced is 'right first time'.

- More effective management using faster production methods, such as encouraging worker **specialisation**. Good managers are at the heart of an efficient business.

> **Key terms**
>
> **Specialisation:** work is divided into separate tasks or jobs that allow workers to become skilled at one of them.

Batch production increases efficiency

Case study

'The switch from job to batch production has allowed unit costs to fall as production efficiency has increased,' said Rashiv Noon, the manager of the Mumbai Dream restaurant. 'Before we extended the kitchen and fitted large cooking vessels and huge ovens, we produced each customer's order separately. Our costs were high, service was slow and although customers loved the food they complained about high prices and long waiting times. Now we produce large quantities of the most popular dishes in advance. Each chef now produces twice as many meals each evening than before the change.'

C *Switching from job to batch production increases production efficiency*

Activities

1 Explain the differences between job and batch production.

2 Explain the efficiency benefits to the restaurant of changing from job to batch production for some of the cooking.

3 Might there be some disadvantages from this change? Explain your answer.

Production and technology

In its simplest form, technology means the use of tools and machines in industry. Small businesses will often need basic technology tools, such as drills and lathes. This chapter is more concerned with more advanced technology, much of it connected with computers and **information communication technology (ICT)**.

Objectives

Understand what technology means.

Understand how technology can make production of goods and services more efficient.

Technology in operations management

Robots

Robots are now widely used in nearly all manufacturing industries. Using robots for this purpose is called computer-aided manufacturing (CAM). The advantages of using robots include:

- Manufacturing robots are known for their speed, accuracy and efficiency.
- They are exact and thorough, achieve high quality, and they do not take breaks!
- They are most frequently used for repetitive, hazardous and boring tasks.
- As they are more accurate than workers, they increase efficiency and reduce waste.

A *Robots increase productivity by performing repetitive tasks quickly and accurately*

Case study

Harry and Farah are skilled carpenters. They make handcrafted tables and chairs that sell for hundreds of pounds each. Apart from sawing and drilling, all the work is done by hand and this is an important part of their business's image. Demand for their products is high. They tried employing another carpenter, but he was not skilled enough. 'Perhaps we should buy a computer-controlled lathe and other tools,' said Harry. 'We could speed up production and supply more customers.'

Activity

Would you advise Harry and Farah to buy computer-controlled machines for their business? Explain your answer.

Computerised stock-control programs

Computerised stock-control programs keep accurate records of goods in stock, goods arriving and goods sold. These are very widely used in service and manufacturing businesses.

These ICT programs can be used to answer these common key questions:

- How much of a product is in stock?
- How old is this stock?
- Which are the fastest-moving items of stock and which are the slowest?

The advantages of using computerised stock-control programs include:

- Automatic stock control, triggering orders when the reorder stock level is reached.

B *Direct computer links to each supermarket branch mean that new orders can be sent automatically when stock levels in shops fall to a certain level*

- Bar coding systems, which speed up processing, recording of stock and customer checkouts.
- Less labour required and fewer errors made, both of which improve efficiency.

Communications technology

Virtually every business will have access to the internet and e-mail. The advantages of this include:

- An intranet system gives rapid and cheap internal communication within the organisation.
- It can be used to improve the accuracy and speed of passing information between the operations management department and other departments of the business.
- The internet allows supplies to be bought quickly from the cheapest supplier online.

However, too much dependence on ICT for communication leads to problems of too many e-mail messages, which can waste workers' time.

Design technology

The advantages of using design technology include:

- **Computer-aided design (CAD)** enables designers to lay their work out on screen, print it out as a 3-D image and edit it.
- New products can be designed and developed more quickly.
- Onscreen simulated designs mean there is no need for physical prototypes, which reduces costs.
- Design data is passed directly to computer-controlled machines for production, reducing the risk of errors and wastage and improving the firm's environmental image.
- Large numbers of different designs of a standard product can be made, which improves the firm's ability to focus on different target markets.

Ania will almost certainly use CAD when she designs gardens for her customers. She can display different design options on the computer screen and make very quick changes in response to customer demands.

Benefits of using new technology:

- Lower unit costs of production as technology replaces labour-intensive methods.
- Better communications.
- Quicker and more flexible operations.
- Better customer service, such as making stocks available as and when needed.

Potential problems of using new technology:

- Cost of purchase can be very expensive and beyond the resources of new small firms. However, almost every business can now afford at least one computer as their prices have fallen in recent years.
- Training of staff is an extra cost, which small firms might find difficult to support.
- Workers can be reluctant to change and accept new ways as they fear they will lose their jobs.

Key terms

Information communication technology (ICT): the use of electronic technology to gather, store, process and communicate information.

Robot: a computer-controlled machine able to perform a physical task.

Computerised stock-control programs: the use of computers to keep records of all stocks and reorder necessary stock automatically.

Computer-aided design (CAD): using computer-based tools to design products, such as buildings, cars and clothes.

Production and quality

What is meant by quality?

A **quality product** does not necessarily have to be the best possible product available. **Customer expectations** will be very different for products sold at different prices. We expect a £1 light bulb to last for at least a year, but we expect a top-of-the-range TV to last for ten years or more. So, we have to be clear from the outset that a quality product does not have to be made with the highest quality materials and to the most exacting standards, but it must meet the consumer requirements for it.

Sometimes a product must meet the highest quality standards and the high cost of it becomes almost insignificant. Internal parts for a jet engine used on a passenger plane will be expected to have a failure rate of less than one in one million. However, if fashion clothing was made to the same exacting standards, how much would a pair of jeans cost? Setting standards too high for a product that consumers do not expect to last for many years can make the product very expensive and uncompetitive.

A *Customer expectations of quality require meals in this restaurant to be prepared to the highest possible standards*

So a highly priced good may still be of low quality if it fails to come up to consumer requirements. A cheap good can be considered of good quality if it performs as expected. Quality is relative as it depends on the product's price and the expectations of consumers.

It is easy to think of quality standards in terms of manufactured goods, such as reliability of cars or the wear rate of clothes. However, quality is a crucial issue for service providers too. Businesses that provide a service are in the tertiary sector of industry.

Objectives

Understand what quality means.

Understand customer expectations of quality.

Key terms

Quality product: a good or service that meets customers' expectations and is therefore 'fit for purpose'.

Customer expectations: the minimum quality standards for a product or service that is acceptable to consumers.

Activities

Sandra bought a new pair of designer shoes for £200. 'I think these will be good value if they last me two years,' she told her friend Kath. 'I paid £15 in a sale for a pair of trainers – I don't mind if they only last a few months,' she replied.

1. Why do you think the customer expectations of these two friends are different?

2. What does this tell you about the meaning of quality?

3. Do they think their products are good quality?

The quality of service offered by UK banks could be measured by:

- the speed taken to answer the telephone
- queuing time in branches
- the number of account errors made
- the quality of financial advice given.

The advantages of producing a quality good or service include:

- More satisfied customers.
- A better reputation.
- Lower costs as wastage is reduced.

■ How can quality be achieved?

Quality assurance is a method of improving quality standards. It works by setting quality standards at all stages in the production of a good or service in order to ensure that customer satisfaction is achieved. It does not just focus on the finished product. This approach means every worker has to self-check their own output against these agreed quality standards. There are a number of advantages of this over the traditional method of checking quality when the final product has been made:

- It achieves high-quality products the first time round, not just inspecting for poor quality.
- Workers should get it right first time, reducing the chances of faulty products.
- Customers should be more satisfied and will complain less.
- Workers are involved in reaching good-quality standards, which is more motivating.
- Components, materials and services bought into the business are checked at the point of arrival.

> **Did you know** ??????
>
> Quality is a relative idea not an absolute one. Quality depends on what customers expect from a product.

> **Key terms**
>
> **Quality assurance:** a system of agreeing and meeting quality standards at each stage of production.

Quality improvements at A Cut Above

Sharon has started A Cut Above hairdressing salon with the aim of making it the best in Scarborough. She employed five staff but was becoming tired of checking up on them all the time. She tried to watch every stylist at work, answer the phone, greet customers and so on. Her sister visited one day when Sharon was away and was shocked at the poor-quality service she received. Sharon decided to call the staff together and she set standards for these aspects of the salon.

- Maximum number of rings before phone answered.
- Maximum time for waiting for an appointment.
- Maximum time between hair wash and cut.
- All customers offered tea or coffee.
- All stylists to spend a minimum time with each customer.

These standards were agreed with all the workers and were pinned up in the salon for all customers to see. Within three weeks the salon was making record profits.

B *Quality is important for service businesses as well as manufacturers*

Case study

Activity

Explain why Sharon's approach to quality seems to be successful.

5.5　Customer service

Do you become annoyed when you are treated badly in shops or banks? Have you ever walked out without buying anything because there was poor customer service? New, small businesses in particular must offer good **customer service** as this will make the real difference between what they offer and much bigger, better-known competitors.

◼ How to offer good customer service

Reliability

The business can open at convenient times, keep appointments with customers, and keep promises such as: 'We can obtain that spare part for your vacuum cleaner by Tuesday'. Customers can be easily lost if small businesses fail to keep their promises and offer an unreliable service.

Pre-sales service

The business can give product advice on the range of options available, the advantages and disadvantages of different models and brands, and an explanation of key terms. This can be particularly important when buying a computer for the first time, for example.

Service at time of purchase

The business should make sure that the product meets customers' needs. Customers often expect different purchasing methods, such as credit or debit card facilities. Make sure that the customer knows how the product works, for example, how to operate the new computer and how to set it up.

After-sales service

The business can provide a helpline or web service to answer important queries about set-up or operation, advice on future product choice, and repairs and maintenance if necessary.

Offering good customer service is an essential part of the modern concept of 'customer relationship marketing', which focuses attention on the importance and profit gains to be made from keeping existing customers rather than spending money on attracting new customers. Alex will quickly establish a good reputation if he keeps all his promises for meeting deadlines for new website designs. Also, if he offers a personal service that meets all customer needs, they will be prepared to recommend him to other businesses keen on establishing their own websites.

Key terms

Customer service: providing services to customers before, during and after purchase, to standards that meet their expectations.

Research activity

Try to find at least two or three businesses that offer after sales services and compare what they offer. Think about why they may offer different services. Try **http://service.hoover.co.uk** as a starting point.

AQA　*Examiner's tip*

Do not confuse customer service with low discounted prices. Many customers prefer good service rather than the lowest possible prices.

◼ The benefits of good customer service

- Customers will return time after time.
- Loyal customers will recommend the business, which will lead to further sales.
- There will be fewer customer complaints, which can be time consuming and expensive to deal with.
- Staff will be more motivated as they are not being complained at all the time.

Bicycle hire shop offers great service

The Dales Bike Hire business is located in some of the most beautiful countryside in the UK. Set up by bike-mad Phil Spencer, it hires bikes to tourists in the Yorkshire Dales. It has just been voted the number one bicycle hire shop in the UK by *Bike Today* magazine. What is the secret of Phil's success?

'I offer an individual service. Many of my customers have come back year after year because they know that I will deal with them personally. After the first enquiry (by post or internet) I contact each customer to find out their exact requirements, such as bike sizes, and special equipment needs like 'kids' bolt-ons' for young children. I quote a fair price and ask for a very small deposit. Final payment is made at the end of the holiday if they are satisfied with the bikes. In two years only one person refused to pay. The bikes are new each year and cleaned after each hire. Any breakdown is reported to me and I either go out myself or send my son. I could open a much bigger store in another town but I am happy to just keep offering a personal service. If we got bigger this might be lost.'

Activities

1. Explain the ways Phil offers a good customer service.

2. Why is customer service a major factor in the success of his business?

3. Do you agree with Phil that this service could suffer if the business expanded? Explain your answer.

A *Good customer service can lead to useful word-of-mouth promotion*

5.6 Consumer protection

Customers are protected by the law when they buy goods or services. Businesses that sell goods and services must know what the most important customer protection laws are. They could experience serious disadvantages if they break these laws, such as:

- bad publicity
- loss of customers
- legal action and the possibility of very heavy fines to pay.

Table **B** details the main laws that protect consumers in the UK.

A Warranties are a way of offering consumer protection

Objectives

Understand that customers are protected by law.

B Main UK consumer protection laws

Law	Main conditions
Sale of Goods Act 1979 and Supply of Goods and Services Act 1982	▪ Goods and services sold to consumers must be as described by the business. ▪ They must be 'fit for purpose' (i.e. they must do the job intended for them). ▪ Goods and services must be of satisfactory quality.
Consumer Protection Act 1987	▪ Compensation must be paid to a consumer who suffers injury or damage to property when correctly using the good.
Competition Act 1998	▪ Businesses must not agree to fix prices at a high level with other similar businesses.
Consumer Protection (distance selling) 2000	This protects the increasing number of consumers who purchase goods over the internet, TV, telephone and mail order. ▪ Firms must give clear information about the good or service. ▪ This information must be provided in writing. ▪ Firms must offer a cooling-off period of seven days for customers to change their minds.
Consumer Protection from Unfair Trading Regulations 2008	▪ Advertisements must not mislead or deceive. ▪ It must be possible for consumers to check price comparisons made in advertisements with other businesses (e.g. by accessing a website).

If consumers were not protected by law, it is likely that they would be taken advantage of by some business owners who just want to make a fast profit and who are not worried about their long-term reputation. It is for this reason, UK laws provide **consumer protection**. This can be both an advantage and a disadvantage for businesses.

Key terms

Consumer protection: laws that protect the interests of consumers when buying goods or services.

The advantages to business of consumer protection laws include:

- Consumers have the confidence to make purchases.
- It reduces the risk of losing customers due to bad products or misleading adverts.
- It prevents unfair competition from low-price businesses that save on costs by selling badly made, dangerous goods.

The disadvantages to business of consumer protection laws include:

- Meeting the conditions of the laws can be expensive.
- Any slight error by the business can lead to legal action and heavy fines.
- It is very time-consuming to keep up to date with new laws on consumer protection.

Which laws are being broken here?

Case study

Bob had started several businesses that had all failed. His latest venture was selling insurance over the internet. He knew very little about insurance. His website claimed to offer 'the lowest prices for car and home insurance' and compared some prices with other insurers. There were no details of how to check on this comparison. Customers had to commit themselves and pay in full by credit card online. If they later changed their mind Bob kept all the money. He met the owner of another insurance website and they agreed not to compete with each other on house contents insurance rates. After six months he proudly boasted that he had not paid out any money to customers who were claiming on their insurances – he always said that they had 'taken out the wrong policy'.

Activities

1 Which UK consumer protection laws do you think Bob is breaking?

2 Do you think consumers need to be legally protected against the actions of people like Bob, who seem to offer low prices but offer such a poor level of service? Explain your answer.

5.7 Impact of ICT on customer service

Technological advances have already been analysed in Production and technology (see pages 78–9). This section deals with how ICT can improve the levels of customer service offered by businesses.

The main ICT applications that have improved consumer service are the internet and business websites. Table **A** outlines the benefits and limitations of the internet for both businesses and customers.

A *Benefits and limitations of the internet to customers and business*

Customers		Businesses	
Benefits	**Limitations**	**Benefits**	**Limitations**
Website is easy to access and contains details of the business and its products.	Customer must have the use of a computer.	It is quite cheap to set up even if business owners cannot design a webpage themselves.	It will need to be updated and this may involve frequent further costs.
It is easy to compare prices and products with other similar businesses.	Websites might not be frequently updated.	Can access consumers around the world and promote the business and products much more cheaply than using traditional means of selling.	Accessing consumers in other parts of the world may lead to communication and transport problems.
Can order and pay for order online from 'the comfort of their own home'.	Goods cannot be tried on or tested before purchase.	It can be a cheaper way to sell most products, rather than opening up a shop or using postal catalogues.	The business must be prepared to reply to e-mails and orders quickly and deal with customers who return goods.
It is easy to contact the business (e.g. by e-mail).	They might not respond quickly and there is no personal contact with sales staff.		

Case study

Daxons decide to close all of its CD and DVD shops and only sell online. The business pays for an attractive and interactive website. Sales increase, but only after Daxons reduces its online prices due to so much e-commerce competition.

Activity

1 Explain the advantages and disadvantages of this decision to:

a customers

b Daxons.

B *A website for a small business*

Ania and Nilesh have much to gain by developing websites for their businesses (see 'Meet the entrepreneurs' in the Unit 1 opener). Perhaps they could ask Alex to design one for each of these businesses? They could be colourful, interactive, provide information about the services these two small businesses offer and give contact details.

e-commerce and global markets

So we have seen that using **e-commerce** and the internet to sell goods and services globally can offer huge benefits, even to small businesses. In fact, for some it might prove to be a cheaper and quicker method of expansion than opening new branches and using traditional marketing methods.

> **Key terms**
>
> **e-commerce:** the buying and selling of goods and services over the internet.

C   *Possible advantages and disadvantages of global marketing using e-commerce*

Possible advantages	Possible disadvantages
The website is open 24 hours a day, seven days a week, 365 days a year. Compare this with the cost of keeping even one shop open all the time.	Customers can walk to a local DVD shop, but how long will they have to wait for delivery from Hong Kong, for example? A long delivery time will damage a firm's reputation for customer service.
Users are not charged by distance. Global consumers using the internet have the same access as local customers. This is unlike telephone marketing.	Some customers doubt whether online businesses actually exist if they are 5,000 miles away. This can lead to customer resistance to purchase or leave credit card details.
Electronic orders and requests for information are almost instantaneous, unlike using the post. This improves customer service.	There may be limitations on the sale of certain perishable goods through e-commerce, such as ice cream!
Cheaper supplies can be bought using the internet. A small business selling kitchen utensils can obtain them from the cheapest world suppliers.	Very small transactions may not be worth the cost to transport them, which can also apply to very large and bulky items too.
It can improve customer service and customer loyalty. For example, the internet can recognise a returning customer and offer a personal welcome. As well as offering competitive prices, the kitchen utensil business can also suggest cookery books and provide links to food retailers.	Selling abroad is not just about having a website. It might need to be available in different languages, which adds to the cost. Some goods and services may be illegal or against the culture of some countries, so changes to the product might be needed if it is to sell at all in some foreign countries.

Dress agency gains a website

Sabrina's dress agency sells good-quality used clothing at prices much below what the articles cost new. Business has been good but she always has more people who want to sell clothes through her shop than customers who want to buy. Her son, Ted, suggested that he set up an internet site for the business. 'If I design a homepage with access to photos of all the clothes you have in stock, you will be able to sell to a much wider market.' Sabrina was not sure, but Ted did a small test site as part of a school project. Hits were slow at coming until a journalist reported the site in a regional newspaper. Now half Sabrina's sales come through the website, but so do half of the returned goods as many customers complain that the sizes are wrong or the photos were misleading. Sabrina decided to keep going with the site, but as Ted was now at university she had to pay someone else to regularly update the product details.

When Sabrina received her first order from a customer in Russia she started to realise the huge potential of e-commerce. Then she wondered how much postage would be and whether she would have to insure the goods during transport.

> **Activities**
>
> **2**   Explain the benefits of the website to Sabrina and her customers.
>
> **3**   Do you think Sabrina should close her shop and just sell over the internet? Explain your answer.

Case study

In this chapter you have learnt:

✔ what production efficiency means and why it is important to businesses

✔ what service businesses are

✔ what quality means to businesses and consumers and how quality products can be produced

✔ the importance of customer service and how levels of customer service can be improved

✔ the importance of technology and ICT in particular to increasing efficiency and improving customer service

✔ why consumer protection laws are necessary.

Case study

The Redgate Conservatory Company is committed to customer service and promises 'the lowest prices of any similar business'. At least, that is what its website says. The facts tell a different story. Sales staff earn a large bonus when they complete new orders. They offer '75 per cent off' discounts, but only after they have doubled the prices first. Deadlines for completion of work are rarely met. Customers who refuse to pay the final payments, which must always be in cash, are threatened with having the whole conservatory removed with no compensation. The sales staff have to travel further and further from Redgate to obtain new business.

The conservatory panels are made in small batches of a limited number of sizes. This keeps unit costs low, but it also means some customers cannot order the size of conservatory they want. They are often promised that 'we can probably make it fit', but it never does.

Activities

1 Identify all the features of poor customer service the company demonstrates.

2 How would you manage this business so that it offered better customer service?

3 Do you think batch production is the best method of production to use in this case? Explain your answer.

4 Apart from the website, explain **two** possible uses of ICT within this business.

Revision questions

1 Which of the following is an example of a product made using job production?
a Mars bars b Ships c Petrol d Sellotape

2 Which of the following is a product that is often made using batch production?
a Computer chips   c Team rugby kit
b Newspapers   d Portrait paintings

3 Which of the following is a benefit of increasing production efficiency?
a More staff and less   c Lower quality
  output   d Fewer computers
b Lower unit costs   used

4 Which of these is an example of improved customer service at a fast food restaurant?
a Lower prices   c Fewer staff
b Fewer menu itemsd   d Different methods of payment

5 Improving quality is a benefit to a business because of which of the following?
a It leads to fewer customers
b It reduces wastage costs
c It reduces output
d Staff turnover increases

6 Which of the following is a frequent effect on a business from the increased use of ICT in operations management?
a More staff are employed
b Production efficiency increases
c More stocks are held
d Fewer different products are made.

UNIT 2   Growing as a business

In this Unit you will learn about how and why businesses grow and the main issues that expansion raises. The work in Unit 2 builds upon the ideas and content introduced to you in Unit 1. Most business owners – but not necessarily all – want their business to expand and become more successful. Expansion leads to a number of questions and potential problems for the owners and the business. These issues include:

- The benefits and risks of growth and the different ways in which businesses expand.
- The legal structure of the business – will this have to change?
- How the objectives of the business change with growth.
- Location – why a good location is important to an expanding business.
- How can growing businesses market their products successfully?
- How can business owners raise the finance needed to pay for growth?
- How can people be managed effectively within an expanding business?
- How can the increasing number of goods or services be produced efficiently?

Unit 2 is split into five chapters:

Chapter 6   The business organisation

This looks at how businesses can grow and how the objectives of larger business might be different to objectives of smaller ones. The benefits and risks of expansion are discussed and examples provided.

Chapter 7   Marketing

Builds upon the marketing ideas you have already studied and applies them to larger businesses. This chapter investigates each component of the marketing mix – price, promotion, product and place. It discusses how large businesses may choose the most appropriate ways to market their products. Finally, how the marketing mix can be changed to respond to market forces is analysed and business examples are explained.

Chapter 8   Finance

In this chapter you will become familiar with the sources of finance available to large businesses. Basic financial statements and calculations are introduced – nothing to worry about, these are explained simply, stage by stage! On completing this chapter you should be able to analyse the content of these financial statements.

Chapter 9   People in business

Efficient and well motivated employees are just as important to large businesses as new, small ones. This chapter introduces the role of the human resources department. It also introduces different ways in which an organization can be structured. The importance of recruiting, motivating and retaining effective staff is made clear – as well as the main ways in which these tasks can be done.

Chapter 10   Operations management

This chapter will allow you to increase your knowledge and understanding of production methods. It explains the importance of organising the production of goods and services efficiently. The possible average cost reductions that can be gained from expansion are explained – as are some of the possible drawbacks to growth that can lead to higher average costs. The important ideas of efficiency and quality assurance are introduced and clearly explained.

6 The business organisation

Objectives

Understand why a business owner may want to expand the business.

Understand the different ways a business can grow.

Understand how business growth can affect stakeholders.

Understand the differences between private and public limited companies.

Understand the objectives that an expanding business might have.

Understand the social costs and social benefits of a business.

Understand the factors that should be considered when relocating a growing business.

What you should already know

✔ The objectives that the owners of a newly formed business might have.

✔ The different legal forms of small businesses.

✔ The importance of the location decision for a new business.

The first chapters of this book studied how new businesses are formed and the decisions business owners or entrepreneurs must take when setting up a new business. The next few chapters study the issues and problems that expanding businesses have to consider if they are to remain successful.

As the following table shows there are many more small businesses in the UK than large ones.

However, a few large firms, such as BP and Tesco, employ more staff than thousands of small firms added together. So large-scale businesses are very important to the economy of the UK in terms of jobs, output and exports.

Some businesses are, of course, much more successful at expanding than others. Some owners really want to expand their businesses, but they fail due to lack of capital, poor management or products that are sold in small markets that are not growing. Compare this with the recent record of ASOS.

A *Number of different-sized businesses in the UK*

Employees	UK businesses 2008
0–4	1,816,230
5–9	377,345
10–19	218,990
20–49	143,350
50–99	48,820
100–249	26,565
250–499	7,775
500–999	2,845
1000+	1,295
Total	2,643,215

Activities

1 What benefits does the business have from being a public limited company?

2 Research the location of Hemel Hempstead. Do you think this is a good location for the new ASOS warehouse? Explain your answer.

3 What benefits might ASOS gain if it continues to expand and increase market share?

Case study

ASOS growth continues despite recession

In a recession most retailers' sales fall. This is not true at ASOS, the online retailer of fashion clothing. It is one of the few businesses that saw an increase in sales in 2008 and 2009. Sales grew by 107 per cent in just six months to September 2008. It is now a public limited company. Four years ago the shares were 5p each and in 2008 they reached £2.82. The Chief Executive, Nick Robertson, is keen for the business to grow further and is planning to sell more top brands as well as own-label clothes. Children's clothing might also be sold.

With no shops to worry about, decisions only have to be taken over where to locate warehouses to stock clothes. The company has just opened a huge new one in Hemel Hempstead, well located to the main UK motorway system.

Adapted from www.guardian.co.uk

Activity

4 Why do you think the Chief Executive wants to expand ASOS further?

6.1 Expanding a business

Many business owners will aim for expansion. Business expansion means that the output and sales increase over a period of time. This indicates that the business owner(s) is running a successful firm – and all business owners like to be thought of as successful!

Survival is the main aim of newly formed businesses. Once the first few risky months and years have passed, business owners will set other objectives too, such as expansion. There are several reasons why the owners or managers might want to expand the business. There will always be some risks involved in business expansion. These reasons and risks are explained more fully in Table **A**.

Objectives

Understand why owners and managers want to expand a business.

Understand the risks of expanding a business.

A *Reasons, benefits and risks of expanding a business*

Reasons for business growth	Benefits	Risks
To increase sales.	This should lead to an increase in profits.	Profits will not increase if the business has had to lower its prices too much in order to sell more.
To increase **market share**.	If the sales of the business grow faster than total sales in the market, its share of this market will increase. This means that retailers will be much more prepared to stock the products of this business.	If other firms are increasing sales at an even faster rate, then market share will fall.
Take advantage of **economies of scale**.	If it is possible to reduce the costs of each item produced as a business grows then is benefiting from economies of scale (e.g. buying materials in large quantities leading to bulk discounts).	It is often much more difficult to manage a large business and this could increase costs of each item produced.
Become more secure and benefit from some customers preferring to deal with large businesses.	It is widely thought that large businesses are more secure than smaller ones. Some customers think that such businesses will be around for the lifespan of the products they are buying.	Large businesses can make losses and be forced out of business too.

Key terms

Market share: the proportion of total market sales sold by one business.

Economies of scale: the reasons why average costs of each item fall as a firm expands.

Reasons for not expanding

Some business owners do not aim for the growth of their firm. The owners may want to keep their firm at its existing size for one of several reasons:

- To keep control – an owner that wants to keep control over all or most parts of the business may decide not to expand it. The larger a business becomes the more likely it is that the owner will have to recruit managers to look after, and take decisions over, different parts of the business.

- To offer a personal service to customers – this is often lost as a firm grows, as the owners no longer know the customers individually.

- To avoid too much risk – expansion means putting more money into the business and this increases the risk the owner is taking.

- To avoid increased worry and workload – both of which come with running a larger business.

Did you know ??????

Rapid growth can end in tears. In an economic recession Starbucks might find it has too many branches that are not making a profit.

B *Rapid growth is one of Starbucks' main objectives*

Activities

1 Look up the number of cafés owned by Starbucks on the company's website. Try to find out how many it owned five or ten years ago.

2 What benefits do you think the business has gained from such rapid growth?

3 What problems has the business had with some of its cafés?

4 Do these problems mean that it has expanded too fast?

Research activity

1 Use the internet to find the UK market share of either a supermarket business such as Tesco, or a car manufacturer such as Nissan.

a How has this market share changed in recent years?

b Why might a higher market share be an advantage to a business such as a supermarket?

c What do you think Nissan could do to try to increase its market share? Explain your answer.

There are two ways in which any business can grow:

■ Organic or internal growth.
■ Inorganic or external growth.

Organic growth tends to be slow and steady, as with John Lewis or Waitrose shops. Franchising is also a form of organic growth. **Inorganic growth** can result in a business almost doubling in size overnight, as with the Lloyds TSB takeover of HBOS bank.

Organic growth

This can be achieved in a number of ways:

■ Open a branch, office or factory in another location.
■ Offer franchises to other businesses.
■ Expand through **internet selling**.

Opening new branches

There are a number of benefits of expanding a business by opening new branches:

■ Slow and steady – organic growth is less risky than taking over or merging with another business. The managers can manage this form of growth more easily.
■ Often paid for from profits – usually, organic growth does not need loans or sale of shares to pay for it. This will reduce the chances of either having to pay interest or lose control by selling shares.
■ Easier to manage and control – when a business expands rapidly by merging with or taking over another business this sudden expansion can be very difficult to handle. With slower organic growth, important decisions can be taken by management with the time to consider all of the risks and benefits carefully. Also, the managers will have experience of the market it operates in – this is not always the case with inorganic growth.

However, this method of expansion also has disadvantages:

■ Too slow for some owners – it can take several years to double the size of some businesses – a merger or takeover could achieve this overnight.
■ Market share could fall – if other businesses are expanding more quickly, market share will fall.
■ No gains from integrating with another business – these are covered in detail in the next section.

Objectives

Understand how a business can expand.

Understand the difference between organic (internal) growth and inorganic (external) growth.

Key terms

Organic growth: expansion from within the business (e.g. by opening more shop branches).

Inorganic growth: expansion by merging with or taking over another business.

Internet selling: marketing products through the business's website.

A The Lloyds TSB takeover of HBOS is an example of external growth, also known as inorganic growth

Activity

1   What advice would you give to the owners of Woodruffs (see page 37) if they wanted to expand their business?

Growth through the internet

Directa Ltd sells industrial products such as safety signs and adhesives. The directors wanted to expand the business. There were no obvious gaps in the product range and they did not want to risk diversifying by selling completely different products. 'As our website was very basic we spent £30,000 on an interactive e-commerce website,' said director Ciaran Crowley. This was much cheaper than buying new premises. New orders came in so quickly from the site that it paid for itself in just one year.

Activity

2   Is it a good idea to expand a business by diversifying and selling completely different products?

Franchises

Business expansion through franchising is very common. The Body Shop and McDonalds are two of the best-known businesses that have used this method of business expansion. Table **B** details the advantages and disadvantages of this form of growth.

B   *Benefits and disadvantages of expanding a business by selling franchises*

Benefits	Disadvantages
Business growth is paid for by the **franchisee** paying fees to use the name and logo of the existing firm. The franchise fee can be an important source of finance for the business.	A franchisee may not keep to their legal agreements (e.g. they could sell products that are not part of the contract). This could damage the brand image of the franchise.
Franchisees are likely to have a high incentive to expand their business quickly.	Most of the profits of each franchisee are kept by the franchisee not the original business.
The management problems of each franchised outlet do not have to be dealt with by the original business. This means that the **franchisor** has fewer staff and fewer management problems than if they owned every branch directly.	If one franchise performs poorly or attracts bad publicity then the whole business could be damaged. A report about dirty kitchens in just one fast-food franchise would be bad for the whole brand.

ChipsAway franchises for sale!

With more than 300 franchisees in the UK alone, this business has expanded rapidly since it was formed in 1994. The business offers a mobile professional car body repair service for small dents and scrapes, costing much less than traditional body repair firms. Each franchisee pays £22,500 for the right to be the sole operator of this service within a geographical area. The head office claims that because each franchisee works for themselves they are motivated to work hard and offer an excellent customer service.

links
www.chipsaway.co.uk

Inorganic growth

This is often called 'external growth' and can be achieved by either a **merger** or **takeover**, which are both forms of 'integration' with another business. There are four different types of integration, depending on whether the other business is in the same industry and/or at the same stage of production. Diagram **D** helps to show the differences between these types of mergers and takeovers.

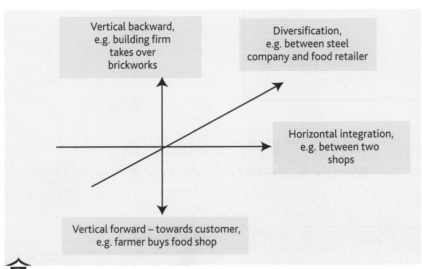

D *Different types of business integration*

Benefits of inorganic growth

It is a rapid form of growth compared to organic expansion.

Horizontal

- **Horizontal integration** can lead to a substantial increase in market share.
- Horizontal integration reduces competition as there will now be one business instead of two.
- Economies of scale are likely with horizontal integration as the firms are at the same stage of production.

Vertical

- **Vertical backward integration** offers reliable supplies of materials. So a jewellery manufacturer could guarantee supplies of gemstones by taking over a mining business.
- **Vertical forward integration** offers a reliable outlet for products. So a furniture maker could obtain a certain retail outlet for its products by merging with a chain of home-furnishing shops.

Diversification

- **Diversification** (also known as conglomerate integration) spreads risk over more than one industry. So while one industry might see a fall in demand, another industry that the business has expanded into might be expanding.

Disadvantages of inorganic growth

- It can be expensive to take over another business – capital raised from loans or shares is usually necessary. Loans will increase interest costs. Selling shares might change the ownership of the company.
- There may be problems of managing and controlling a much larger business, especially one that is growing so rapidly.
- With vertical integration and diversification, management may lack experience of these other businesses, the products they deal with and the markets they sell in.

AQA Examiner's tip

The advantages and disadvantages of each form of inorganic growth are not all the same. Be prepared to refer to the different types of inorganic growth.

Activities

1. Classify each of the following possible takeovers:
   - BMW takes over Mercedes.
   - British Airways takes over an in-flight catering business.
   - HSBC bank takes over a publishing business.
   - Nokia takes over a business producing microprocessors for mobile phones.

2. Would you advise Levi Strauss to take over a large chain of clothing stores in the UK? Consider all of the possible advantages and disadvantages of this company operating its own stores before coming to a final decision.

E Panasonic is planning to take over Sanyo – will consumers lose or gain from this?

Research activity

1. Research a recent merger or takeover in the UK. Try using the website business pages of a quality newspaper, such as *The Times* or *The Daily Telegraph*, or the BBC business website.

a What are likely to be the major benefits to the businesses concerned?

b Could there be some disadvantages to the businesses?

c How will workers and customers be affected?

6.3 Conflict between stakeholders

Business growth will affect stakeholders in different ways. Some stakeholder groups may react to protect their interests if they consider that business expansion could damage them. Table **A** analyses the advantages and disadvantages of business growth to different stakeholder groups.

A *Impact of business growth on different stakeholder groups*

Stakeholder group	Possible benefits	Possible drawbacks
Owners	There should be a higher level of sales and profit.	If the owners are the managers as well, there might be more responsibility and stress.
Workers	There might be more opportunities for promotion and, possibly, greater job security.	There may be job losses if jobs are duplicated in a merger or takeover as only one person is needed for that job. Shareholders will expect costs to be cut.
Customers	Prices may be lower. The larger firm can benefit from economies of scale if it can insist on lower prices from suppliers.	Prices could rise. With a merger or takeover, there might be fewer competitors, so the business could raise prices.
Suppliers	More orders might be received from the larger business.	The expanding business may insist on lower prices from suppliers as it is now a more important customer. It could even threaten to cancel contracts if suppliers do not lower prices.
Bank	Lending more finance to the expanding business makes this a more profitable account.	There may be increased risks for the bank. If a bank loan is used to pay for growth and expansion is not successful the firm might not be able to repay the debt.
Government	Strong and expanding businesses pay more tax to government.	If a **monopoly** is created then the public interest could be at risk.

B Tesco has expanded its sales by 30 per cent in four years – will all of its stakeholders benefit from this?

Stakeholder groups will often take action to defend their interests. They want the growing business to meet their objectives as much as possible. Table **B** explains how these groups can respond to business growth.

C *Ways to defend stakeholder interests as the business expands*

Stakeholder group	Ways to defend stakeholder interests
Workers	■ Try to stop any job losses following merger or takeover. ■ Use trade unions to negotiate the best possible settlement for workers who do lose their jobs. ■ Negotiate for higher pay, as expanding businesses may become more profitable. ■ Put the case for internal recruitment, encouraging existing workers to gain from jobs with more responsibility in the bigger business.
Customers	■ Check prices carefully following expansion – are cost savings being passed on? ■ Use consumer groups and their websites to put pressure on larger firms to offer good value to consumers.
Suppliers	■ Insist on reasonable prices for products supplied and prompt payment. However, this might not be effective if the large business threatens to use other suppliers. A small supplier to a large business may be in a weak position.
Bank	■ Keep a close watch on the firm's bank account. Is the loan or overdraft limit being reached? ■ In some cases the bank might ask for a senior manager to sit in on the firm's Board of Directors meetings.
Government	■ Government will be concerned if a merger or takeover creates a monopoly. The Competition Commission can be asked to investigate and might recommend that a merger or takeover be stopped.

Case study

The Competition Commission is going to investigate the merger between IBS OPENSystems and Capita Group plc, which are just two of three firms that supply specialist accounting software to local governments. The Commission will look into whether the merger should be prevented if it reduces competition too much.

In contrast the Competition Commission was told not to investigate the Lloyds TSB takeover of HBOS. The government suggested that fewer but stronger banks were good for the public interest.

Activities

1 The government is just one stakeholder affected by expanding businesses. List four others affected by the merger of the software companies.

2 Do you think the Competition Commission should stop all merger and takeovers that create a monopoly? Explain your answer.

Lloyds and HBOS form UK's largest bank

Case study

The 2008 credit crunch gave Lloyds TSB the opportunity to take over HBOS (Halifax) for a much lower price than would have been possible even a year before. The new bank will have nearly 30 per cent of all UK bank accounts – the largest UK bank by far. Some branches will be closed in towns where both banks currently have branches and cost savings from up to 40,000 lost jobs will help to boost profits. Some managers hope that £1.5bn could be saved each year. One of the two head offices will be closed. Some consumer groups are worried about less choice of banks, fewer branches and possible worse customer service. HBOS customers may feel their money is more secure in a larger bank. The government encouraged this merger as it wants UK banks to be strong and stable, despite there being less competition.

Group research activity

Use the internet to find out more about the Lloyds TSB takeover of HBOS. A team of students should represent each of the stakeholder groups, presenting the advantages and disadvantages to their group. Stakeholder groups could include: Lloyds TSB managers; HBOS managers and staff; bank customers; government; town councils where the banks have branches.

6.4 Choosing the right legal structure

When starting a business the two most common legal structures are sole trader and partnership.

As a business expands other types of legal structure become more common. In the UK nearly all large or medium-sized businesses (over 250 workers) are **limited companies**. There are two types of limited company:

- **Private limited company**
- **Public limited company**

As a sole trader or partnership business expands it requires more capital. This could be obtained by taking on further partners. However, many investors are reluctant to invest in a business that offers them no **limited liability**, especially if they are not going to control it or take decisions about its operations. The most common solution to this problem is to create a limited company. This is nearly always, at least initially, a private limited company.

Case study

The Redford Building partnership has three partners. Recent large construction work had left the business short of capital to buy more machinery and hold more stocks. The three partners asked other builders if they would be prepared to become partners in Redford. They all refused. One said: 'The business is profitable at the moment, but during a recession it could fail and then I would be, with the other partners, liable for all the debts of the business. It's too risky for me.'

The three partners converted the business into Redford Building Co Ltd and many friends in the building trade were keen to buy shares in the company when offered them.

Activity

Explain why friends of the three original partners were prepared to buy shares in the company, but had not been interested in becoming partners.

A *Advantages and disadvantages of a private limited company*

Advantages	Disadvantages
Has more status than a sole trader or partnership. Some customers and suppliers will have more confidence in the business as it has a clear legal identity.	Cannot be listed or quoted on the Stock Exchange so cannot offer shares for sale to the general public.
Attracts private investors known to the owners to buy shares in it by giving them limited liability.	Scope for expansion into a really large business is limited.
Original owners often remain as directors and senior managers so they will continue to run the business.	Share prices are not quoted daily so **shareholders** cannot be sure what their shares are worth.
Limited liability for all shareholders, unlike the unlimited liability faced by sole traders or partners in a partnership.	Accounts are available to the general public at Companies House so it is possible to find out how a private limited company is performing.

Objectives

Understand the differences between a private limited company and a public limited company.

∞ links

See Chapter 1 for further information on sole trader and partnership structures.

Key terms

Limited company: a business recognised as a legal unit that offers investors (shareholders) limited liability.

Private limited company (Ltd): a company that cannot sell shares to the general public. It is not listed on the Stock Exchange.

Public limited company (plc): a company able to sell shares to the general public by being listed on the Stock Exchange.

Limited liability: investors (shareholders) in a limited company can only lose their investment in the business if it fails; they cannot be forced to sell assets to pay off the firm's debts.

Shareholders: part owners of a limited company – they own shares in it.

The main disadvantage to a private limited company is that it cannot raise substantial sums of capital from large numbers of people or investing firms. If the owners of the company want to do this to pay for further growth the business has to be converted to a public limited company.

B   *Advantages and disadvantages of a public limited company*

Advantages	Disadvantages
Able to raise substantial capital for expansion by selling additional shares.	The original owners often lose control as a high proportion of shares are sold. Is this risk worth the extra finance raised?
Higher status than a private limited company. It will attract more publicity as it has thousands of shareholders who want to read about the company's performance.	Professional directors and managers appointed to run the business may have different aims to those of the shareholders.
Share prices are listed by the Stock Exchange so shareholders can work out the value of their shares. They can buy additional shares or sell those they own easily. This is not so easy for shareholders in private limited companies.	Must disclose all main accounts to the public. These are often greatly publicised in the media, with much more public scrutiny than with private limited companies.
Limited liability for shareholders, as for private limited company shareholders.	Company can be taken over if a majority of shareholders agree to a bid from another business.

C   *Richard Branson is the owner of the Virgin group of companies – these are some of the largest private limited companies in the UK*

D   *As a plc this business could be open to take over bids*

6.5 Changing business aims and objectives

Unit 1 outlined the main objectives of small businesses as:

- survival
- profit
- growth.

What are likely to be the objectives of an expanding business? How will they change from those of a small firm? The main danger for small and newly created businesses is lack of cash. This causes many such firms to fail in the first few months. This is why survival is the main objective of new firms. Once a business has survived it should be more secure and have a reasonable cash flow. This means that the owners and directors can start to set other objectives for the expanding business. Table **A** considers the main aims that are often set for growing businesses.

Did you know ??????

During a recession the need to survive might become the main objective of even large businesses.

A *Objectives for expanding businesses*

Objective	Explanation
Profit growth	If the company is still controlled by its owners (as with most family-owned private limited companies) profit will still be a main aim. Profit will be used to pay dividends to shareholders and invest back in the company to achieve further growth.
Increasing market share	Once a business has survived after the first risky years, the owners/directors can start to focus on increasing market share. This will: ■ increase the status and reputation of the business ■ give the business more power over retailers and suppliers ■ give the firm more control over prices and may lead to the firm becoming the main or dominant firm in the industry.
Increasing shareholder value	This is a common objective of public limited companies. The directors will want to keep their jobs by keeping shareholders happy. Increasing shareholder value means: ■ share price rises over time ■ increased **dividends** can be paid out to shareholders.
Managerial objectives	In large public limited companies the thousands of shareholders appoint directors to control the business. These senior managers are not the owners of the business – they may own some shares but not a majority of them. They may have their own objectives for the business they control. This **divorce between ownership and control** means that the directors may aim to: ■ increase their status by running a larger business ■ increase their salaries and 'perks' ■ gain publicity from well-publicised decisions, such as takeovers and expansion abroad.

Key terms

Dividend: payment made to shareholders from company profits – usually made annually.

Divorce between ownership and control: when directors control a public limited company and thousands of shareholders own it, but the two groups may have different objectives.

Case study

The first few months of operating the City Catering business had been touch and go. The mobile catering service offered by business partners, Sheila and Imran, had been very successful with companies that were too small to run their own staff canteens. The problem was, the partners had paid for all food supplies in cash, but had to wait up to six weeks to be paid by companies. Survival was therefore the vital objective. After two years, the couple had built up a good reputation and their suppliers offered them four weeks to pay. Cash flow became less of a problem as business customers paid regularly, and City Catering even had a cash surplus. Imran wanted to take most of the cash out of the business to increase his and Sheila's salaries. Sheila was keen, however, to spend the capital on expansion: 'If we can buy another van and employ more staff we will increase sales, so future profits will pay our higher salaries!'

Activities

1   What other objectives could the partners set for their growing business?

2   Do you think expanding a business such as this will always lead to higher profits? Explain your answer.

Expansion leads to change of objectives

Case study

The owners of the Computer Training Co Ltd were, at first, just interested in business survival. For three years after the business was formed they just managed to pay all of their bills. As the company became better known, the owners Bill and Shikenda opened new branches paid for from rising profits. After ten years they had 12 branches open offering training courses to the public and other businesses. They decided to form a public limited company and sold some of their own shares to make some real money for themselves.

Activity

3   How have the objectives of the owners of this company changed as it has grown?

Activities

In 2008 Marks & Spencer set the following objectives:

- Continue to expand sales by investing in more stores.
- Expand the international business.
- Increase sales from the M&S Direct business.
- Integrate the environmental objective of 'being carbon neutral' into all aspects of the business.

4   Why do you think it is important for Marks & Spencer to have objectives for the next few years?

5   How could it check to see if these objectives have been met?

6   Find out the objectives of another large or expanding business by investigating its website.

AQA   Examiner's tip

If answering a question about business objectives you should check to see if it is a newly set-up business or a well-established, expanding business.

B   Marks & Spencer

6.6 Social costs and benefits

Ethical and environmental objectives

Is profit the main measure of business success? Should there be a wider view taken of what firms are in business to achieve? Increasingly, business managers are setting **ethical** and **environmental** objectives for their firms as well as growth and profit targets. Sometimes this is because they have values and beliefs other than the aim of making money. In other cases though, managers just understand the importance of image and how the business appears to other groups in society. This means managers are considering not only whether a decision will lead to a profit or not, but what impact it could have on society and, as a result, the image of their business.

Changing objectives

Firms are now adopting objectives other than those based on profits, growth and shareholder value for a number of reasons:

- Laws on environmental protection have become stricter. To break such laws would lead to heavy fines and bad publicity for a company. This has led to many firms having environmental objectives.
- There is growing and widespread public support for action against dumping waste and climate change – one of the **social costs** of business activity. Businesses with clear environmental objectives often gain good publicity and consumer loyalty.
- Consumers are putting pressure on firms to be increasingly ethical. They are demanding more organic foods and low-polluting cars, and not buying products made in ways that they find unacceptable, such as clothes made in low-wage 'sweat shops'.

Being ethical can *reduce* short-term profits:

- Paying wages above the minimum set by the law is more expensive in the short term than paying workers low wages in cash, so that no records are kept. However, would it be right to pay workers below a certain level?
- Not paying money bribes or giving gifts to win a contract can mean lost sales. This can be very significant in some countries where bribery and corruption are accepted ways of doing business. However, would it be right to offer a bribe to gain an order?
- Not forcing suppliers to reduce prices further, if it means they go out of business, in the short term can mean paying slightly more than other firms who do not care if suppliers are driven out of business. However, would it be right to push supplying firms to the brink of extinction?

Objectives

Understand what social costs and social benefits are.

Understand why many businesses now consider these important when setting objectives.

A Marks & Spencer has an environmental objective to be carbon neutral by 2012 – plastic bags will have to go!

Key terms

Ethical objective: a business aim to 'do the right thing' according to the values and beliefs of managers, even if this is not the most profitable way (e.g. pay workers in low-wage countries above average rates).

Environmental objective: a business aim to protect the environment during its operations (e.g. to recycle waste water). This will reduce social costs.

Social costs: the costs of business activity, including both financial costs paid by the firm and the costs on society (e.g. factory pollution).

Activity

1 In groups think about some ethical companies that you may know and discuss how they are both similar and different.

Being ethical can *increase* long-term profits:

- Other ethical firms will want to do business with ethical companies as it reflects well on them too. The Cooperative Bank refuses to accept any investments from companies in the tobacco or weapons industries. However, it has attracted many thousands of new accounts from customers who like this approach.

- Workers may be more motivated if they are well treated and well paid. It may be easier to recruit good workers if they know they will be well treated. Microsoft has no problems in recruiting some of the best software engineers in the world as they are treated as valued members of the organisation.

- The government is more likely to give contracts to ethical firms or those with high environmental standards that offer **social benefits** as it wants to set a good example.

- Consumers may avoid unethical firms and spend more with ethical ones. Consumers can boycott firms that are shown to be acting unethically.

- Suppliers will develop a good relationship with a business that treats them fairly. They will offer the best terms possible and put this customer first in the case of a shortage of supplies.

Did you know ??????

Acting ethically or with high environmental standards can cost the business a lot in the short term, but it can also lead to long-term profits.

Key terms

Social benefits: the benefits of a business activity, not just to the firm but to society (e.g. new jobs created by business expansion).

AQA Examiner's tip

Ethical and environmental objectives may look good to consumers and suppliers, but is the firm really setting these objectives because the managers believe in them or just to make the company look good? You should consider this point in an answer.

links

www.amway.co.uk

Amway's social and ethical aims

Case study

Amway is one of the world's largest private limited companies. It is a direct selling organisation marketing 450 consumer products, such as cosmetics and food supplements. It aims to be profitable, but it also has a wider vision: 'to help people live better lives'. At the heart of this commitment is the One by One Campaign for Children that helps disadvantaged children from around the world. Amway supports its employees in putting time and money into support groups for poor children to gain access to education and medicines.

In addition, the company aims to use sources of renewable energy, change products and packaging to become more biodegradable, offer employment and job security to workers and good value to consumers.

Activities

2 What are the likely costs and benefits to a company like Amway of having social as well as profit objectives?

3 Do you think a chemical manufacturing business should have ethical and environmental objectives? Justify your answer.

6.7 Location

The location of any business is important as it will affect its costs, revenue and image. An ideal location would be one that:

- minimises costs
- maximises revenue.

This ideal location would prove to be very profitable! The main problem with this simple approach is that the cheapest locations will often lead to low sales – unless the business sells over the internet, whereby customers do not have to see the cheap location for themselves.

The factors that managers of a growing business will consider when choosing a location include:

- Cost of the site – the cost of buying the premises, such as a shop or a workshop, or the cost of renting. For shops, some of the most expensive sites such as in city centres can also be the most profitable.
- Labour costs – these can vary from region to region. If it is possible for the business to locate in an area with low labour costs then this would be an advantage, unless the firm needs high-income local consumers, such as a shop selling expensive handmade chocolates.

A Steel works tend to be located close to sea ports for ease of transport of heavy raw material

- Transport costs and proximity to suppliers – if heavy raw materials are used in production, such as in steelmaking, the business will have to pay high transport costs if suppliers are a long distance from the location. Businesses that need a lot of specialist suppliers might locate close to these firms. So IT industries in the UK are heavily concentrated together in the Thames Valley as they provide each other with components and specialist services.
- Sales potential – the sales of a growing business might depend on being situated in certain locations even if the land and rent costs are high. So high-class dress retailers are found in some of the most expensive locations in all of the UK's major cities.

■ Managers' preferences – in small businesses, the owners or senior managers may have a preference for one location over another. It may be more attractive to live there because there are better schools or leisure facilities, for example.

Rolls-Royce opts for quality location

Choosing the lowest-cost location for the Rolls-Royce factory was not a priority. When BMW moved production from the industrial northern town of Crewe it chose one of the most crowded and expensive parts of the country, South East England. The Goodwood factory has many advantages but low cost is not one of them. One of its benefits is that it is close to a small airport where the helicopters and executive jets of intending purchasers of Rolls-Royce cars can arrive in style. Buyers who might be interested in a Rolls-Royce are invited to visit the factory and attend events held at the nearby exclusive marina and horse and motor race courses. The area has been coined a 'playground for the wealthy' and future customers often spend a day or two at the races or a morning at the marina before browsing the cars, and then signing an order form!

Adapted from www.timesonline.co.uk

Case study

B *Selfridges department store in Birmingham*

For many years the world-famous department store Selfridges had just one branch in Oxford Street, London. It then opened a second branch in Trafford Park in Manchester and another in 2003, in the Bull Ring in Birmingham. It has chosen expensive city-centre sites and is now looking at other sites around the country to support its expansion programme.

Case study

Activity

2 Suggest a UK city where you think Selfridges could open a new and profitable department store. Why have you chosen this city?

6.8 Location – go global

In recent years many well-known UK-owned businesses have located in other countries, sometimes closing most of their UK operations at the same time. One of the main features of **globalisation** is the growing trend for businesses to relocate completely to another country or to set up new operating bases abroad. Electrolux is a typical example.

Objectives

Understand the reasons why some UK businesses decide to locate in other countries.

Case study

Electrolux factory to close in Durham

An Electrolux cooker factory in Durham is to close, with the loss of 500 jobs. It has been making increased losses. Only three years ago the company believed this was still the best location for manufacturing cookers and invested £7m in the plant with the aid of a government grant of £1.6m. Now the company believes that the exchange rate and wage and other cost pressures make it uncompetitive and have decided to switch production to a factory in Poland. It has estimated that it can make a profit making only half the machines in this new factory than it did in the UK.

Adapted from www.bbc.co.uk

This process is often referred to as **off-shoring**. The world's largest corporations are now virtually all **multinationals**.

Key terms

Globalisation: increasing trend for goods to be traded internationally and for companies to locate abroad.

Off-shoring: making products or parts of products in other countries. Services can be off-shored too, as with telephone call centres moving to India.

Multinational: a business with operations in more than one country.

Possible benefits of locating aboard

- Lower site or land prices – London is the second most expensive city in the world to buy office space in, after Tokyo. Locating in other countries, such as Poland or Chile, would cost much less. However, it might not be as convenient and it could increase transport costs back to the 'home' country.

- Lower labour costs – for many businesses that use a lot of labour, such as telephone answering services or clothing manufacturing, the cost savings from employing staff in low-wage countries can be huge. However, will the quality of the product be as good as before?

A *Labour costs around the world*

Country	Weekly pay (€)
India	25
China	41
Bulgaria	43
Brazil	60
Hungary	159
Germany	750

Federation of European Employers, January 2008

B *Labour costs are lower but is it ethical to relocate to open a factory such as this?*

- Avoid trade barriers – the three main Japanese car makers all have factories in the UK. One of the main reasons for locating in this country was that cars made here can be exported to the rest of the European Union with no controls put on them, such as tariffs. However, will the UK factory workers be as productive and well-motivated as Japanese ones?

- Take advantage of fast-growing economies and markets – both the Chinese and Indian economies have grown on average by more than 10 per cent a year for ten years. The UK economy (up to 2009) had expanded by 2.5 per cent a year over the same period. There may be many more chances to increase sales in countries other than the UK. However, will goods and services have to be changed to meet consumer tastes in other countries and will this be expensive?

Possible problems of locating abroad

- Language differences may make communication with workers difficult.

- Transport costs will increase if the goods are shipped back to the UK. These costs must not be bigger than the cost savings of locating abroad.

- Bad publicity might follow this location decision because of the local UK jobs that will be lost. It could be looked upon as an unethical decision, which could damage sales in the UK.

- If the company moves to low-wage countries it might be claimed that it is taking an unethical decision. If the company has strong ethical values this may be a very important factor.

AQA **Examiner's tip**

When discussing a decision to locate in another country you should be prepared to look at the possible disadvantages as well as advantages to the business.

Case study

John Pearce, the Chairman of Burberry, the world-famous clothing manufacturer, defended the decision to close its factory in Wales. The clothes that used to be made in this factory will now be sourced from China. 'The Wales factory was not commercially viable … it is now possible to source some products from overseas at a significantly lower cost.' The company hopes to expand sales in Asia.

The decision to close the factory has left the brand facing worldwide protests. Protests and demonstrations organised by the GMB trade union have been supported by the singer Tom Jones and the Manchester United boss, Sir Alex Ferguson.

A Welsh MP insisted that Burberry should not import clothes from Bangladesh or the Philippines as minimum wage levels were so low and that the company should also check that child labour was not employed in its suppliers' factories overseas.

Adapted from www.guardian.co.uk

Activities

1. Outline **two** possible benefits to this company of its decision to move production to China.

2. Outline **two** possible disadvantages to Burberry resulting from this decision.

3. Do you think Burberry's decision was unethical? Justify your answer.

Most small businesses sell one main product. For example, hairdressers sell haircuts, florists sell flower arrangements and garden designers sell garden designs.

As businesses expand, it is common for them to extend the range of products that they sell. So a small garage may start to sell second-hand cars as well, and a publishing firm might also offer website design services. If a firm is selling more than one main product it has a **product portfolio** or **product mix**.

■ Product portfolio

There are a number of benefits of selling more than one product.

- To offer a wider range of goods and services to support the original product. The florist may offer a variety of pots and vases for the flower arrangements so that the customer spends more in any one visit.

- To attract new consumers by aiming at a different **target market**. An electrical store might start to sell computer games and games consoles to attract younger consumers who would not normally buy lights and plugs.

- To **diversify** so that if sales of the original product decline, increasing sales of new products might replace it. A confectionery shop selling quality chocolates that have seasonal demand could start to offer homemade ice creams, both of which sell well at different times of the year.

Very large businesses often have very large product portfolios to offer customers a huge range of goods and services. For example, Tesco's portfolio includes groceries, electrical goods, insurance, clothing and petrol. John Lewis's portfolio includes furniture, carpets, beds, clothing and restaurants.

There are also a number of problems of having such a large product mix.

- Many managers have to be employed to take decisions about the products.

- Bad publicity for one product may harm the company's whole image.

- The cost of developing and selling so many products is high.

- Some products may fail if the company has not done sufficient market research.

■ Product life cycle

Table **A** shows the pattern of sales over the lifespan of a typical consumer food product, which is called the **product life cycle**. It can be split into four stages:

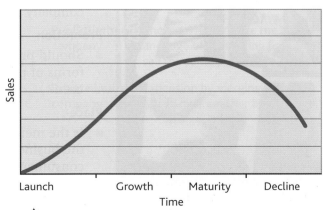

A typical product life cycle

- Launch – sales may start slowly as consumers get to know the product.
- Growth – sales accelerate if it is well advertised and if consumers like it.
- Maturity/saturation – sales level off as competitors enter the market or tastes change.
- Decline – sales fall as it becomes less popular. It may eventually be taken off the market.

How extension strategies can impact other departments

Extension strategies can be used to extend the lifespan of a product, but they can have an impact on other departments of the business. Examples include:

- Updated designs – such as the iPod nano. However, this will need expensive research and development by the production department.
- New advertising campaign – Cadbury's 'gorilla drummer' advert for Dairy Milk, for example. However, the finance department may be asked to increase funding for more advertisements.
- Targeting new markets with an existing product – such as promoting sports clothing as 'street wear' or selling the same product in foreign markets. However, selling abroad may need people with foreign language skills to be employed to market the products.
- New brand image – Lucozade is now marketed as a sports' drink not a beverage for the ill. However, this may also require a change of packaging and expensive new advertisements.

Did you know ??????

Some products remain on the market for many years, such as Marmite and Ovaltine. These products are often re-launched or have expensive promotion campaigns to interest new generations of consumers.

Key terms

Extension strategies: steps taken to extend the life cycle of the product.

Did you know ??????

These examples of extension strategies show the link between marketing decisions and other parts of the business.

Research activities

1 Find out which company makes Kit Kat and list the other products it produces.

2 Why does it produce a range of products?

3 How has this firm used extension strategies to extend the life cycle of Kit Kat over the years?

B *Have a break …*

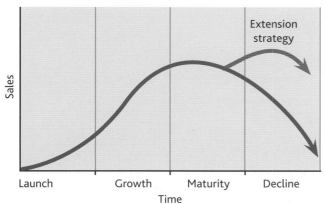

C *This shows the effects of an extension strategy on sales*

Marketing mix: price

Price is a very important part of the marketing mix. It affects:

- whether people can afford the product and how quickly the business's sales will grow
- how competitively it is priced compared to rival products – a business that is competitive is more likely to grow
- the product's image – high price often means high quality to many consumers. Setting a low price for Sony TVs, for example, might actually reduce the chances of business growth.

During business growth, pricing decisions will be based on four main factors:

- degree of competition
- nature of the market
- costs of production
- loss-leader pricing.

◼ Degree of competition

If the market is very competitive then if the business is to grow by increasing sales it may have to reduce prices equal to or below those of competitors selling very similar products. This is called **competitive pricing**.

◼ Nature of the market

If it is a market for exclusive designer clothes or advanced IT equipment where consumers expect to pay high prices to maintain the image of the products, **price skimming** might be used. This means setting a high price and once the product starts to face competition, prices can be reduced.

If it is a mass market where similar products are sold to large numbers of consumers then a low or **penetration price** might be used. Sales growth will only come from low prices. Once the market share objective has been reached, prices can then be raised.

Objectives

Understand the different ways of setting the price for a product.

ASDA, the UK's second biggest supermarket group, launched a new price war by cutting the prices of 5,000 products. The company's aim is to have more low prices than any other major supermarket group.

Adapted from www.timesonline.co.uk

Key terms

Competitive pricing: setting a price for a product based on prices charged by competitors.

Price skimming: setting a price at a high level to create a high-quality and exclusive image.

Penetration pricing: setting a price at a low level to gain greater market share.

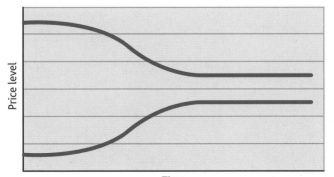

Price level

Time

Skimming pricing

Penetration pricing

 The difference between penetration and skimming pricing

Costs of production

Growing businesses need profits to invest back into the business. Prices of products have to cover all costs if profits are to be made. Adding a profit mark-up to the unit costs of making a product will achieve this. This is called **cost-plus pricing**.

Loss-leader pricing

Making a deliberate loss on a product which will be cancelled out by profit from the sale of other items is called **loss-leader pricing**. It is widely used in two main ways:

- Supermarkets commonly sell popular items, such as milk or sugar, at below cost price to attract customers to buy these goods. Once in the store it would be rare for customers not to buy other products too. This achieves sales growth for the supermarket and the sales of the other items cancel out the loss on the loss leader.

- Manufacturers sell one basic product cheaply, below cost, hoping to sell supporting items profitably. Electronic equipment such as games consoles or computer printers are often sold very cheaply in the hope that profits will be made on the sale of games or peripherals, such as ink cartridges.

B   *The HP Deskjet D1500 printer costs £20, but the replacement ink cartridge costs £18*

Key terms

Cost-plus pricing: setting a price by adding a profit mark-up to the total cost of producing a product.

Loss-leader pricing: setting a price below cost hoping to gain other profitable sales.

Did you know ??????

Many factors can influence the final price decided on for each product. The importance of each factor will vary from product to product.

Research activity

Research the prices either of designer fashion wear from a well-known label or of the latest Bentley car model. Which factors influence the prices charged for these products?

Activities

1. If a furniture manufacturer makes a table costing £200 and wants to make a 15 per cent profit mark-up, what will the price of the table be?

2. Research the prices of five branded grocery products in at least three different supermarkets. Which supermarket was cheapest overall? Why do the other companies not lower their prices further?

Promotion has several important roles to play in marketing a product:

- informs consumers of new products
- creates a brand image and a sense of identity
- supports other marketing decisions, such as a reduction in price
- helps a business to achieve sales growth

Methods of promotion

Growing businesses are most likely to use the following methods of promotion.

Advertising

Advertising can inform consumers about new products or can create new interest in established products. Adverts with celebrities or those filmed in expensive locations can help to create an exclusive image for a product, which will help support high prices.

Sales promotions

Sales promotions include games, competitions, special offers and buy-one-get-one-free deals. They encourage consumers to buy more of a product or to choose this product rather than a competitor's.

> In 2008 Dr Pepper offered a free can of drink to every US citizen – vouchers can be downloaded from their internet site, which have to be taken to a retailer. The company hopes that the free publicity the offer has generated will increase short-term sales.
>
> www.brandrepublic.com

Direct marketing

Direct marketing tries to contact consumers without going through other media such as television. E-mail, telemarketing and direct mail are all good examples of this. Sales made through these methods would be directly due to this contact being made and a result of advertising. For example, Dell uses mail drops and newspaper leaflets to communicate directly with potential computer buyers, who are encouraged then to buy directly from the company's website.

Selecting the promotional mix

Some firms use more than one form of promotion. Cadbury's uses television and newspaper adverts, shop point-of-sale displays, sales promotions such as 'sports gear for schools' and sponsorship. There are various factors that affect the choice of promotional mix.

Cost and affordability

Some forms of promotion are very expensive and some growing businesses with limited resources cannot afford them.

A *This was one of the most watched adverts of 2007/2008 – it increased sales of Dairy Milk by more than 7 per cent*

Nature of the product

A business selling robots to manufacturers will not use the same promotional mix as a business selling leather furniture to consumers. Business to business (B2B) marketing tends to use trade fairs and specialist industrial magazines as its main forms of promotion, as it aims to focus directly on business customers not retail consumers.

The Paris Air show held in July is used by makers of civil and military aircraft to display their products to airlines and governments from all over the world. These products are not advertised on television or radio!

Nature of the market

If the market is very local or if all of the customers are well known to the business, the need for extensive advertising is much reduced. Direct marketing would be much more appropriate in these cases. When the market is spread over a wide geographical area and the identities are unknown, then advertising and sales promotion become more common.

Competitors' promotions

Generally, if competitors spend a large amount on an extensive promotional mix then this will lead to a business doing the same.

> **Case study**
>
> Marks & Spencer used taxi advertising in London as part of its campaign to raise consumer awareness of its female clothes range. The brightly decorated taxis also supported the womenswear television advertising campaign featuring top models. Marks & Spencer UK sales for the 13 weeks of the campaign were up 10.4 per cent with clothing up 10.7 per cent.
>
> www.taxipromotions.com
>
> **Activity**
>
> 1 Why do you think it is important to keep a record of sales changes during a promotion campaign?

Research activities

1 Use the internet to find out how much a well-known business spends on promotion or how much is spent on promoting one brand. **www.marketingmagazine.com** often has articles about promotion costs.

2 Which forms of promotion does this company or brand use?

3 Why do you think it uses these forms of promotion?

■ Sponsorship

By giving money or resources to support an activity or event, such as a sports competition or a music concert, a business can gain a very large amount of publicity. Sponsoring events that are televised will potentially send the business name into millions of homes. Barclays Bank sponsor the English Premier League and Harvey's the furniture retailer sponsor the TV programme, Coronation Street. If an event failed or received bad publicity then this would also look bad for the business that sponsored it, however.

Did you know ??????

It is important to remember that 'promotion' does not just mean 'advertising'.

Although the cost of television advertising fell to an average of £4.81 per 1,000 adults for a 30 second commercial in November 2008, that still makes a half minute advert during *The X Factor* a cool £48,100!

Adapted from www.telegraph.co.uk/finance

Coke Zero is sold globally and had a $75m advertising budget in 2006 including a sponsorship deal with *American Idol*.

www.usatoday.com/finance

Gap does not advertise on TV yet spent $400m on promotion – about 3 per cent of total sales in 2007. This is the average proportion of sales spent by retailers.

www.bnet.com/retail

Did you know ??????

Many firms use more than one type of promotion at the same time – they can support each other to make sure that as many consumers as possible 'get the message'.

Activity

2 Next time you are watching TV or at an event see how many sponsors you can notice.

In the marketing mix 'place' means the channel of distribution used between the manufacturer and final consumer. There are five main channels of distribution.

Producer–retailer–consumer

This route is commonly used by food companies selling through large supermarkets and by furniture producers selling through furniture stores.

This route would be appropriate for a growing business when it wants to cover a bigger market than just local consumers. Retailers hold stocks of the product and arrange for appropriate presentation and demonstrations of the product. The producer would have to offer discounts to the retailer.

Producer–wholesaler–retailer–consumer

This route is commonly used by food producers aiming to sell to widely dispersed convenience stores, and book publishers selling books worldwide.

This route would be appropriate for a growing business that had limited finance and wanted the cost of holding stock and transport to retailers to be paid for by another business. The producer would have to sell the goods at a discount to the **wholesaler** though.

Telesales

This route could be used to sell products to other businesses, for example, magazine advertising space, IT services, or directly to consumers. **Telesales** is commonly used by double-glazing firms, insurance companies and kitchen renovation firms. The main problem they face is consumer resistance to 'cold calling' – ringing on the chance of someone being interested, using a pre-prepared script.

This route would be appropriate for a growing business that could not afford a large sales team or expensive-looking retailing space.

Mail order

Mail order is used by many clothing firms, such as ASOS, and insurance companies selling, for example, house and car insurance. It is most appropriate for a growing business when the product being sold can be well presented on a paper leaflet and when consumers can be targeted. For example, only sending mail shots containing a toy catalogue to families with young children.

A *Some companies may use telesales as a channel of distributions*

Internet selling

This is the most rapidly growing distribution channel in the UK. In October 2008, when retail shop sales fell by an average of 5 per cent, sales over the internet rose by 15 per cent. It is used to sell a huge range of goods and services, from clothes to cars, and holidays to bank credit cards. It can be particularly appropriate for a growing business. This is because, although an interactive website is essential, the costs of operation are low compared to setting up a retail shop. Also, as it is a form of direct selling with no middlemen or intermediaries, the business does not have to give discounts to wholesalers and retailers.

Case study

Online sales boom as shoppers desert high street

Out of every £1 spent by British shoppers, 17p is now going to online retailers. Consumers are now switching away from traditional shops in favour of picking and paying at their home computer. A new survey shows £26.5bn was spent on the internet in the first six months of 2008, up 38 per cent on 2007. The credit crunch is keeping people away from shopping centres but not their computers. While John Lewis's department stores have been hit by the downturn its online operation is growing rapidly. Ocado, which delivers Waitrose groceries, reports sales up 25 per cent on a year ago and Mothercare saw internet sales increase by 28 per cent in just 15 weeks. Analysts expect the trend to continue with tight household budgets, the high cost of petrol and 'a general wish to shift to more sustainable shopping patterns'. According the IMRG analysts, 56 per cent of people think that buying online is more environmentally friendly than high-street shopping.

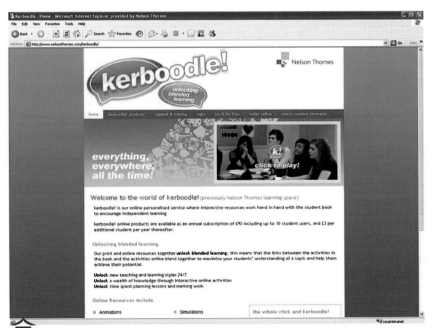

B *Website design is important to successful online sales*

AQA Examiner's tip

Selecting the 'right' distribution channel. If you are asked a question about choosing the 'right' channel for a product think about: convenience for customers, distance of the business from customers, the cost of holding stocks and whether customers are likely to have access to the internet.

Activities

1 Explain **two** reasons for the growth in online sales at a time when shop sales are falling.

2 Would you advise some businesses to shut their shops and just sell online? Explain your answer.

3 Are there any disadvantages to consumers from buying online?

Group activity

PlayIT is an expanding business, making computer games and consoles for teenage consumers. You have been asked to advise it on the best methods of distribution for its products. In groups, research how similar companies, such as Eidos and Nintendo, distribute their products. Present your group's view on how PlayIT should distribute its products to the class.

Large and growing businesses can raise finance or capital in several ways. Sometimes only one source of capital is used, while on other occasions several methods are used. Choosing the appropriate source is an important business decision. The main methods of raising finance are detailed below.

Objectives

Understand the main sources of finance for large or growing businesses.

Understand which methods of finance are appropriate in different cases.

Retained profit

Retained profit is a form of internal finance as no outside banks or other lenders are involved. When a business makes a profit that it does not pay to shareholders in dividends, it keeps (or retains) it in the business.

> **BP is profitable**
>
> In the financial year ending 2007, BP plc recorded retained profits of $12,739bn. This internal source of finance is essential to allow the company to invest in new refineries and search for more oil.
>
> *http://spectator.advfn.com*

Selling unwanted assets

This is another form of internal finance as it turns the business's own property and assets into cash. The business has to make sure that it does not need the assets – if it does, then it could arrange a **sale and leaseback** deal.

> **Major bank raises finance by selling offices**
>
> HSBC bank has agreed to sell and lease back its Canary Wharf office building. It will raise £1.09bn of finance for the bank, but there will be annual leasing charges to pay.
>
> *http://hsbc.com*

A   *HSBC headquarters in Canary Wharf are no longer owned by the bank*

New share issue

The legal structure of a company, as explained in Chapter 3, allows this type of business to raise capital by selling further shares. Selling shares can be expensive as advertising in the national press and using specialist financial advisers to help with the share sale will be costly.

> **Huge issue of shares for EU's largest bank**
>
> In November 2008, Santander, the largest EU bank, planned to raise £5.9bn from the sale of shares. The bank had planned to sell some of its assets. Property prices were falling, so it decided to raise finance from shares instead.
>
> *www.bbc.co1/hi/business7719859*

Loan

Borrowing from a bank of another financial institution is external finance. Any loan adds to the debts of a company, as interest must be paid monthly or yearly and eventually the loan has to be repaid. Loans can be short term, for example, to pay for an increase in stock for the next three months. Long-term loans, say for five years, could be used to buy new equipment.

■ Mortgage

A mortgage is a long-term loan used to buy property, such as a factory or office space. The loan is secured with the property purchased. This means that if the business cannot pay the loan back, the bank or lender takes over ownership of the property.

■ Which source of finance is best?

This depends on many factors. Table **B** explains when each source of finance is most likely to be used, its benefits and possible disadvantages.

> ### Yell has £3.7bn debt mountain
>
> Yell, the telephone directories group owes nearly £4bn. The money was borrowed to pay for the takeover of directories companies in Spain and the USA. Now the firm is talking to its banks to extend the loan. The interest rate might rise from 7 per cent to 9 per cent.
>
> *http://business.timesonline.co.uk*

B *The advantages and disadvantages of different sources of finance*

Source of finance	When most used	Benefits	Disadvantages
Retained profits	For long-term expansion.	▪ No interest and does not have to be repaid. ▪ No loss of control to new owners/shareholders.	▪ Many businesses may expand but still not be very profitable. Profits may be too low to finance growth. ▪ When profits are low business growth will be slow so loans or share issues might be better options.
Selling unwanted assets	To pay for expansion or to pay off debts.	▪ No interest paid and the finance raised does not have to be repaid. ▪ No loss of control of the business.	▪ The asset is no longer owned. ▪ The asset may still be needed by the business so there will be leasing costs.
Share issue	To pay for long-term expansion (e.g. buying another business).	▪ No interest has to be paid. ▪ Share capital does not have to be repaid.	▪ Dividends will be expected by shareholders. ▪ May be loss of control by original owners.
Loan	For short- or long-term purposes (e.g. to buy machinery or to pay for increases in stock).	▪ Overdraft is very flexible – can be varied on a daily basis up to an agreed limit. ▪ No loss of control by existing owners. ▪ Lower interest rate than overdraft or unsecured loan. ▪ No loss of control by existing owners.	▪ Interest costs may be high. ▪ Must be repaid – this could be at short notice if the bank is worried about the future of the business. ▪ Property is used as security – will be given up by business if debt cannot be repaid. ▪ Interest costs.

Activity

1 For each of the following cases where a business needs finance, suggest and explain **one** appropriate source of finance.

a A toy shop wants to buy more stock in the months leading to Christmas.

b A car manufacturer plans to take over a smaller car maker.

c A department store wants to expand by buying a large city-centre shop premises.

d A steel company closes a large iron and steelworks but plans to expand and modernise another site.

Purpose of financial statements

All businesses must keep financial records. If they did not managers would not know:

- whether a profit or loss is being made
- how much cash is flowing into and out of the business
- when suppliers must be paid for goods and when tax must be paid to the government.

These financial records will include details of:

- products sold, the value of them and which customers have not yet paid
- goods and services bought by the business, the value of them and which suppliers have not yet been paid
- equipment and other assets purchased
- wage and other labour costs.

At the end of each financial year important statements will be prepared by the firm's accountants. This chapter explains what these statements are and what they contain. They help the stakeholders in a business answer two important questions:

1 Is the business trading at a profit or a loss?
2 How much is the business worth?

Without answers to these two questions:

- shareholders or owners will not know whether to invest more into the business
- banks will be uncertain whether to lend more or to demand repayment of earlier loans
- government will not know how much tax the business should pay
- workers will be uncertain about jobs and whether the business can afford to pay higher wages.

Main financial statements

Profit and loss account

The **profit and loss account** contains six important pieces of information:

- **Sales revenue** – the value of sales revenue will increase when the number of units sold increases, or the same number of units is sold at a higher price.
- **Cost of sales** – this is the bought-in value of the goods sold by the business plus labour costs needed to make the good or provide the service.
- **Gross profit** – this can be increased either by increasing sales revenue or by reducing cost of sales, such as buying cheaper materials or reducing labour used.

Key terms

Profit and loss account: this shows whether the business made a profit or loss over the last period (usually a year). It is also known as the income statement.

Sales revenue: the value of goods sold.

Sales revenue = number of goods sold × price

Cost of sales: the cost to the business of the goods sold.

Gross profit: the difference between sales revenue and cost of making the products sold.

Gross profit = sales revenue – cost of sales

Overheads: expenses of the business that are not directly part of the production process (e.g. rent and management salaries).

Net profit: the difference between sales revenue and total costs of the business.

Net profit = gross profit – overheads

- Expenses or **overheads** – these will include the fixed costs of the business.
- **Net profit** – this is a very important profit calculation. It shows how successful the managers have been at making a profit once the total costs of the business (cost of sales + overheads) have been subtracted from sales revenue.

Activities

These are the profit and loss figures for Acme Builders Ltd for 2008.

Sales revenue earned from building work	£115,000
Cost of materials used	£35,000
Cost of labour	£55,000
Overheads including rent and interest costs	£15,000

1 Calculate the gross profit.

2 Calculate the net profit.

Interpreting profit and loss accounts

Look at the gross and net profit figures in the case study of JJB Sports plc. How successful was the business in the first six months of 2008? Was the company more or less profitable than during other time periods and than other businesses? In the six months to August 2008, its closest competitor increased sales by 19 per cent to £300m and net profit by 54 per cent to £12.4 million (**www.guardian.co.uk**). Which company performed more successfully during this period?

The best way to analyse accounts is to make simple comparisons between two results. These are called ratios. The most widely used profit ratios are:

- **Gross profit margin** – a business can increase this margin by either increasing price or reducing the cost of sales, that is making a higher profit on each £ of sales.
- **Net profit margin** – a business can try to increase this margin in a number of ways, but they all have possible problems. For example, an increase in price will raise the net profit margin but will customers still buy the product? The cost of sales can be reduced by using cheaper materials, but will customers notice a change in quality? Finally, a reduction in overheads would increase net profit margin, such as a cut in advertising, but would this lead to lower sales?

Activities

3 Using the earlier figures for Acme Builders Ltd, calculate the gross profit margin.

4 Calculate Acme Builders Ltd's net profit margin.

5 In 2008 Redgate Builders Ltd's gross profit margin was 20 per cent and its net profit margin was 10 per cent. Compare the profitability of this company with Acme Builders Ltd.

6 Suggest three ways in which Acme Builders Ltd could increase its profitability.

JJB Sports: simplified profit and loss account
For six months ending 27/7/08

Sales revenue	£344.7m
Cost of sales	£166.49m
Gross profit	£178.21m
Overheads	£177.21m
Net profit	£1.0m

www.jjbcorporate.co.uk

AQA Examiner's tip

You will be expected to be able to calculate gross and net profit from simple figures. You should also be able to explain the difference between these two profit figures.

Key terms

Gross profit margin: the percentage of sales revenue that is gross profit.

Gross profit margin % = (gross profit ÷ sales revenue) × 100.

Net profit margin: the percentage of sales revenue that is net profit.

Net profit margin % = (net profit ÷ sales revenue) × 100.

AQA Examiner's tip

Don't worry about remembering these two formulae – they will be given to you in the exam if you are expected to use them!

Balance sheets

Balance sheets show the value of what a company is worth. If the company owns a higher value of assets than the value it owes as liabilities, the difference is called 'shareholders capital'. There are several different types of assets and liabilities. Just to confuse matters, they are sometimes called different names, depending on the date the accounts were drawn up. Table **A** shows a simple **balance sheet** for a limited company, highlighting some of the traditional terms used to describe its **assets** and **liabilities**.

A A balance sheet for Hurtwood Computers Ltd

Balance sheet as at 31/12/08 £000		Explanation
Fixed assets	225	These are now known as non-current assets. These are items owned by the business with a lifespan of more than one year. Buildings, equipment and machinery are the most common types of fixed assets.
Property	150	
Equipment	75	
Current assets	32	These are assets owned by the business that are either in a cash form or are likely to be turned into cash within one year. Stock may include raw materials, components and finished goods.
Stock	20	
Debtors	10	
Cash	2	Debtors: the value of goods sold to customers that have not been paid for yet.
Current liabilities	24	Current liabilities: short-term debts of the business – they will have to be repaid within one year.
Creditors	20	
Overdraft	4	Creditors: the value of products supplied by other businesses that have not been paid for yet.
Net current assets	8	This figure is very important – if the business has short-term debts greater than current assets it may have difficulty paying these debts.
Total assets less current liabilities	233	This is the total value of assets owned by the company minus its short-term debts.
Creditors falling due after one year	(100)	Creditors falling due after one year: these are debts that will eventually have to be repaid, but not within one year. Also known as long-term loans or liabilities.
Bank loan	(100)	
Net assets	133	Value of assets after all liabilities have been subtracted.
Capital and reserves	133	Shares issued: value of shares bought by shareholders.
Shares issued	33	
Retained profit	100	Retained profit: profit kept in the business after tax and dividends have been paid.

Interpreting balance sheets

Balance sheets can also be analysed using ratios. You will need to know how to calculate two ratios. Both of these indicate the **liquidity** of a business.

Current ratio = current assets ÷ current liabilities

For Hurtwood Computers Ltd this would be: 32 ÷ 24 = 1.33

This is a safe current ratio result as it is more than 1. This means that for every £1 of current debts or liabilities, the company has over £1 of current assets to pay them back. If the current ratio result was much lower, such as 0.4, the business could only pay 40 per cent of its current liabilities from current assets. If all of the suppliers and banks asked to be paid at the same time, the business could not do it!

Acid test ratio = (debtors + cash) ÷ current liabilities

For Hurtwood Computers Ltd this would be: 12 ÷ 24 = 0.5

For this company, this is an acceptable acid test ratio result. This ratio is a tougher test of liquidity and always gives a lower result than the current ratio. It excludes stocks, which are not very useful for paying debts as they have to be sold first and this could take ages. If an acid test ratio is below 0.25 for example, it means that the business has very little cash either in the bank or just about to be received from customers to be used to pay short-term debts. Some businesses will expect to have a higher acid test ratio – for example, a shopkeeper who always pays his bills in cash.

Activity

1 These are the balance sheet figures for Redgate Furnishers Ltd at 31/12/08.

Debtors	£16,000
Creditors	£28,000
Stocks	£22,000
Cash	£2,000
Overdraft	£24,000

a Which of these terms are assets?

b Which of these terms are liabilities?

c Calculate the current ratio.

d Calculate the acid test ratio.

Case study

Has BP got enough liquidity to pay its short-term debts?

The following information is taken from BP plc's accounts for the year ending 31/12/07. The data has been simplified to make it easier to understand. (All figures US$ million.)

Current assets		Current liabilities	
Stocks	26,554	Creditors	43,152
Debtors	38,020	Short-term loans	15,394
Cash	3,562		

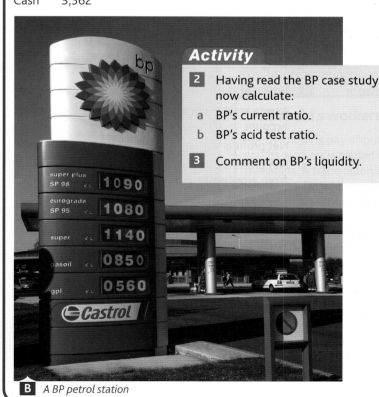

Activity

2 Having read the BP case study now calculate:

a BP's current ratio.

b BP's acid test ratio.

3 Comment on BP's liquidity.

B A BP petrol station

AQA Examiner's tip

The current ratio and acid test ratio will be given to you in the examination if you are asked to calculate them. However, you will still have to know what the result means and the problem the business will be in if the results are very low.

9.1   Organisational structure

◼ Why do businesses need an internal structure?

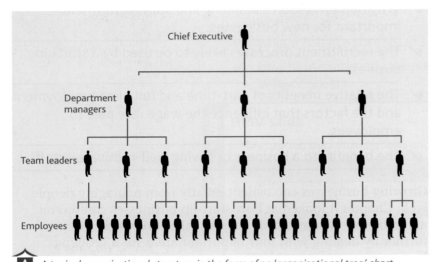

A   A typical organisational structure in the form of an 'organisational tree' chart

There are a number of benefits to business of having an **organisational structure**:

- Makes clear who is responsible for which department and which workers.
- Makes clear who workers should communicate with and take instructions from.
- Makes clear how many different departments and **layers of management** there are.

The example used in Diagram **A** has some key features:

- There are four layers of management, also known as 'levels of hierarchy'.
- Each manager is responsible for three people – this is called a '**span of control** of three'.

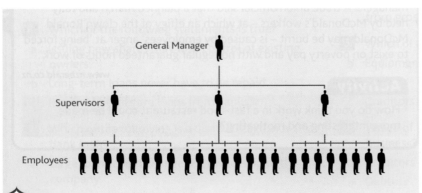

B   A flat organisational structure

Objectives

Understand why businesses need internal structure.

Understand how this structure can affect how a business is managed.

Understand the benefits and challenges of centralisation and decentralisation.

Key terms

Organisational structure: the internal links between managers and workers showing lines of authority.

Layers of management: the number of different levels of management and responsibility in a structure.

Span of control: the number of junior employees each manager is directly responsible for.

Activity

1   Think about the structure in your school – how does it relate to these organisational structures?

The organisational structure shown in Diagram **B** has only three layers, so it is a *flat* not a *tall* organisational structure. The span of control of the three senior managers is eight. This gives a wide span of control.

C Benefits and appropriateness of both types of structure to a growing business

Flat organisational structure – wide span of control	Tall organisational structure – narrow span of control
There should be quicker communication through the business as there are fewer layers for messages to pass through.	It is easier to control fewer staff so managers can closely supervise quality.
More responsibility is given to each manager and worker as senior managers cannot control everyone's work all the time.	Responsibility is kept in the hands of senior managers so there is less risk of workers taking wrong decisions.
Workers may need training to take responsibility, which could increase their level of motivation.	Training costs will be lower as workers will not have to be trained in how to take responsibility and decisions.
Appropriate for senior managers who believe that workers should be more involved in taking decisions and responsibility.	Appropriate for senior managers who believe that workers need to be controlled and told what to do.

■ Centralisation and decentralisation

Some business managers think that all important decisions should be taken by them at the centre of the organisation, at Head Office, for example. Other managers think that some decisions should be taken by managers and workers away from Head Office. Table **D** details the benefits and challenges or limitations of both approaches.

D Benefits and challenges of centralisation and decentralisation

Centralisation	Decentralisation
Senior managers have full control, taking decisions for the whole business, but no ideas or suggestions come from other staff.	It gives power to junior managers and workers and may motivate them, but they will need training to be able to use this power effectively.
In times of a crisis centralised decision-making should lead to strong leadership and quick decisions, but this can be used as an excuse for using central decision-making all the time.	Local managers may have better knowledge than senior managers in Head Office (e.g. which products would be most popular in different areas of the world), but it may be expensive to put different decisions in place in different divisions.
Decisions are taken for the benefit of the whole business not one division or department, but divisions or departments might not be able to take quick decisions that could benefit the whole business.	Junior managers are given experience of decision-making and taking responsibility, which will prepare them for senior roles, but poor decisions by junior managers could harm the whole business.

Key terms

Centralisation: senior managers take all important decisions.

Decentralisation: decision-making power is spread to managers in branches and divisions of the business.

Activity

2 In just one year, from November 2007, Tesco opened over 100 new-style convenience Fresh & Easy grocery stores in California. This was the first time the UK-based company had opened shops in the US. Explain whether you think the following decisions should have been taken centrally in London or decentralised to Tesco managers in California.

a Which goods to sell.

b The prices to charge.

c The total amount to be spent on this US expansion.

Recruiting the best workers

The likely benefits to a business of recruiting the best workers for each job include:

- high productivity – the best workers will be efficient
- high-quality output or customer service – the best workers will be keen to make sure that high quality is maintained
- higher profits resulting from these first two benefits
- workers will be less likely to leave as they will be doing a job that they are good at.

How to recruit the best workers

There are four important stages in the **recruitment** process:

Job analysis – finding out exactly what the job involves. This will clearly help when selecting the best people. This stage of the process must find out:

- The exact tasks and duties of the job – for example, a hotel receptionist must welcome guests and work out their bills when they check out.
- The skills – for example, the receptionist must be able to use IT and telephone systems.
- The training that might be required, such as in customer service and calculating customers' bills.
- How a person's work will be analysed and appraised, such as by hotel guest feedback or 'mystery guest' visits.

A **job description** is the making up of an explanation of the job vacancy. This will be used in advertisements for the job vacancy and to tell people interested in the job what will be expected of them. Table **A** shows an example of a job description.

A *An example of a typical job description*

General information	Sales Manager – head of South Eastern division.
Content of the job	To be responsible to senior managers for the performance of the sales team in the South Eastern division.
Working conditions	Based at Head Office. Level 2 salary band. Six weeks holiday.
Information on performance	Appraisal based on sales performance compared to targets.

A **person specification** is the explaining to people interested in the job what qualities and skills are expected from the successful applicant. The person specification would include sections such as qualifications needed, expected skills gained, useful personal qualities and relevant interests.

Using either **internal recruitment** or **external recruitment** – a job vacancy can either be filled by trying to recruit someone who already works for the business or by attracting someone from outside of the business. Table **B** shows the claimed benefits of both methods.

B

Benefits of internal recruitment	Benefits of external recruitment
Gives existing workers a chance of promotion or an opportunity to do another job. This should provide motivation and an incentive to do well.	Gives much wider choice of potential applicants.
The workers will not need any induction training as they know how the company works.	External candidates could be better qualified and of higher quality.
The skills and personality of internal candidates should already be well known.	Prevents breaking up existing teams within the business and avoids jealousy created by an internal candidate being promoted over the heads of other workers.
Should be quicker and cheaper than recruiting externally.	Avoids creating another vacancy in the business that will then have to be filled.

Selection of new workers

Once people have applied for the vacancy, selection of the best candidate must take place. This can be done in several ways:

- Application form and personal details – these will be used to decide who to call for the next selection stage.
- Interview – this allows managers to see, in person, how the person is likely to fit into the business and how they respond to some challenging questions.
- Testing – many firms now use some form of testing during the selection process. This can include aptitude and personality tests. These are meant to be more accurate than the personal impressions gained from an interview alone.

C *The quality of staff is important to businesses*

Activities

The Imperial Hotel in Brighton wants to recruit a new senior chef to replace a chef who is retiring. The manager of the hotel wants to recruit the best chef available to control staff, supplies, ordering and quality. He has undertaken a detailed job analysis with the retiring chef and the catering manager. He now has to prepare a detailed job description and person specification. The hotel manager would like to recruit internally as young workers often complain about lack of promotion prospects. The catering manager is looking for an external recruit to improve the current standards in the kitchen.

1 Prepare a sample job description and person specification for this post, similar to the one shown on page 134.

2 Would you advise the hotel to recruit externally? Explain your answer.

Staff training

There are several benefits to a business from training workers:

- Workers are more able to cope with changes, such as advances in technology (e.g. new IT equipment).
- Increased productivity and efficiency of staff – for example, by allowing them to become more flexible and able to do a range of different jobs.
- Reduced chance of products being of poor quality.
- Staff will feel that they are being invested in and will gain additional skills. These benefits might encourage staff to stay in the business and may increase their motivation.

Training has costs too:

- The financial cost of training courses can be greater than the benefits obtained from them.
- Workers are often not producing whilst they are being trained.
- It might be more difficult to keep or retain trained employees as they could find it easier to find higher paid jobs in other firms.

Types of training

Induction training

Induction training includes learning what the business does, who does what within the business, health and safety procedures and the role and tasks of supervisors.

Benefits: Helps new workers feel part of the company 'team', reduces risk of accidents through ignorance, makes the worker feel more familiar with the business and the key personnel within it.

On-the-job training

On-the-job training is often undertaken by watching and helping other workers as they perform similar tasks. This has the benefit of directly learning very relevant information from skilled workers in-house, but not involving any cost of taking the worker away from the place of work.

On-the-job training requires a tutor with the correct skills and knowledge. This sometimes does not exist and training is not to a sufficiently high standard.

Off-the-job training

Off-the-job training can be organised either by the company, if they take workers away from their jobs to a training facility, or by a specialist training company, employed by the business for this purpose. It is beneficial if the company lacks experienced trainers and/or there is no one with the specific knowledge and skills that can be taught by outside specialists.

Objectives

Understand the advantages and disadvantages of different types of training.

Understand how and why businesses use a staff appraisal system.

Key terms

Induction training: initial training to familiarise new recruits with the systems of a business.

On-the-job training: takes place when employees receive training as they are working at the place of work.

Off-the-job training: takes place away from the job at another place (e.g. the business's training centre or a college).

A Workers receiving on-the-job training in a factory

This form of training takes workers away from the factory or offices which means they can do no work, even though it might be a busy time for the business.

Key terms

Appraisal: assessing how effectively an employee is working.

Case study

The Excel Sports Centre has recently opened a new gym and health suite. It has recruited four new members of staff. They are all qualified gym instructors – two have just passed their exams and two worked for other sports centres. Excel managers did not let them take any responsibilities or lead any fitness classes until they had all been through a lengthy induction training programme.

Activities

1 Explain **four** items that should be included in this induction training.

2 Do you agree with Excel managers that this training is very important? Explain your answer.

3 Should the training take place within the sports centre or at a local college? Explain your answer.

Staff appraisal

How do managers know that workers are doing well or not? Are workers contributing as much to the business as they could? These questions can be answered by using a system of **appraisal**.

Appraisals are usually done by managers senior to the workers. Interviews are often used after the worker has filled in a detailed questionnaire about how well they think their performance has met targets. Appraisals offer these benefits:

- Provide feedback to the worker – how they have performed since the last appraisal and whether previous targets have been met.
- Make suggestions for improving performance.
- Increase motivation, as workers will feel that an interest is being taken in them.
- Set worker's objectives for the future – these should be agreed with the worker.
- Identify training needs and potential for promotion.
- Provide a basis for pay increases, or not if the appraisal is negative.

There are three main methods of appraisal:

- Superiors – the worker's senior manager assesses performance based on their knowledge of the recent work done.
- Self appraisal – individuals carry out an assessment of their own work and progress, which can then be checked and agreed with a superior.
- Peer appraisal – carried out by work colleagues at the same level within the organisation. Some staff may be unwilling to appraise fellow workers though.

Case study

The Imperial Hotel recruited a chef externally after an interview and a cooking demonstration. The new chef was given the following targets to work towards:

- Low staff turnover in the kitchen.
- Low food wastage rate.
- Low levels of customer complaints.

After six months, all was not going well. Three out of six kitchen staff had left and 20 per cent of food was thrown away since the new chef had been selected. However, the customers loved the new menu and the quality of food.

Activities

4 How successful does the new chef seem to have been?

5 Would you advise the hotel manager to appraise the chef's performance? Explain your answer.

6 The chef complains that he has never been trained in record keeping or managing staff. What form of training would you recommend for the chef?

Motivating and retaining staff

▪ Benefits of motivated workers

When workers are keen to work they are said to be **motivated**. A business will benefit in several ways from having motivated workers:

- Increased productivity and efficiency of workers – workers will be motivated to work well even without close control by supervisors.
- Improved quality – workers will be keen to produce quality goods and provide excellent customer service.

All these benefits should reduce costs and increase profitability. There are three main methods managers can use to motivate and retain their workers.

Staff training

The general view is that when a business offers well-run and appropriate training opportunities to staff, there will be a significant increase in motivation. Untrained staff often feel they have low value and low status in an organisation, and they may not work well because of this.

Styles of management

The way people are managed can have a great impact on their motivation levels. Two extreme management styles are **autocratic** and **democratic**:

- Autocratic – workers may not be motivated as they must respond to all orders without question; they are not involved in decisions and are not trusted.
- Democratic – if workers are well trained they will be able to contribute to decisions. This should motivate them to work hard for the business.

Objectives

Understand the methods a business could use to motivate and retain employees.

Key terms

Motivated: the will to work due to the enjoyment of the work itself.

Retaining staff: keeping existing staff in the business, which cuts down the cost of recruitment, selection and training.

Autocratic management: managers who believe in taking all decisions and just passing instructions to workers.

Democratic management: managers who involve workers and less senior managers in decision-making.

Did you know ??????

There is no one correct style of management. Even democratic managers have to operate in an authoritarian style at times.

Case study

A huge fire wrecked Brown's Bakery. Jim Brown was a popular manager who normally gave his workers many opportunities to take decisions. This morning was different. He rang all of his workers the morning after the fire and gave them clear instructions of what they should do. Some were asked to ring suppliers and customers to explain the problem. Others were instructed to contact estate agents to look for other suitable buildings. Jim's finance manager was told to contact the insurance company. Within three weeks the bakery was operating again from a refurbished building – no customers and suppliers had been lost permanently.

Activities

1. Which style of management did Jim use after the fire?

2. Was this the appropriate method? Explain your answer.

Remuneration methods

Which method of paying employees is most likely to motivate them to produce high-quality output at high-output levels? Perhaps it depends on the individual worker. A student working as a part-time employee may be motivated by different factors to a senior manager employed by the same business for 15 years. Any comments about pay methods and motivation must therefore be rather general ones. Table **A** shows four common pay methods, their main advantage and disadvantage, and the possible impact they could have on employee motivation.

A *Advantages, disadvantages and impact of different methods of pay*

Pay method	Main advantage	Main disadvantage	Possible impact on motivation
Piece rate – a fixed amount for producing each unit of work	Should lead to higher output if workers are only motivated by the chance of earning more money.	May lead to poor quality if workers rush jobs just to increase output.	Assumes workers are only interested in pay. Some may be motivated by job security, social factors, the chance of promotion and recognition by management.
Hourly wage rate	Workers can calculate how much they should receive each day or week.	Does not provide any direct incentive to increase output or put in extra effort.	Provides more pay security than piece rate, which is important to most workers. It also encourages staff to work overtime.
Salary – fixed annual sum, paid monthly	Provides pay security – workers know exactly how much they will receive each month.	No direct link between daily effort and pay. Works best with an appraisal system to determine salary level for the next year.	This is the most commonly used pay method for permanent managerial staff, so when offered to other workers it gives status and security. If annual appraisals are used, workers may work hard to achieve annual targets so that a higher salary might be offered.
Profit sharing – a share of annual profits is given as a bonus in addition to basic pay	Makes workers more responsible towards the company and keen to help it increase profits.	What happens when a loss is made? There might be some lack of pay security, such as during a recession.	May help to keep staff in the business if they consider that profits are likely to increase. Should have a positive impact on long-term responsibility and motivation.

Links between pay methods and management style

Democratic managers would encourage staff training and would be likely to use salaries and profit sharing. Autocratic managers would cut costs by using minimum employee training and use piece rate to ensure that workers keep busy and increase output.

An executive of BP has criticised the firm's management. He said that workers at the bottom of the hierarchy are not listened to. In addition, senior managers were too authoritarian and did not listen well.

http://newsvote.bbc.co.uk

Case study

Activities

3 Which style of management is the BP manager criticising?

4 Explain whether workers are likely to be motivated by this style.

Flow production

The production methods used by small businesses have disadvantages.

- Job production can be slow and only suitable for small levels of production.
- Batch production takes time to switch between different batches and can lead to high stock levels. For example, batches of school uniforms may only be produced once a year and some of the stock will be held for this length of time before another batch for this school is produced.

The alternative operations methods used by many growing and large businesses are known as **flow production**.

The main features of flow production

- Large-scale production – the cost of the equipment needed for flow production is only worthwhile if output is large, such as the cost of robots in car production.
- Standardised product – the key features of the product being made do not change although some changes in colours and extras are possible. For example, the basic structure of a washing machine will be the same on one production line but certain design features might be different between models.
- **Specialisation** – the workers and the machines used in flow production are often specialised in one task. This allows much faster work to be done. For example, workers will tend to focus on one aspect of computer assembly.
- **Division of labour** – the complete job is divided up into a large number of small tasks. This allows specialisation and each task can often be done by a machine very rapidly.

Objectives

Understand how flow production operates, its advantages and disadvantages.

Understand how lean production methods can lead to efficiency.

Key terms

Flow production: large-scale production where each stage of production is carried out one after the other, continuously, on a production line.

Specialisation: work is divided into separate tasks or jobs that allow workers to become skilled at one of them.

Division of labour: breaking a job down into small, repetitive tasks that can be done quickly by workers or machines specialised in this one task.

Case study

ACME International makes bathroom units. After introducing flow line production methods its output became closely linked to demand. With batch production it used to make units even if they had not yet been ordered by customers. Flow production changed all that. Non-productive time has been cut – workers are continually busy and not waiting for a previously started batch to work through, stocks have been reduced to minimum levels and the faulty product rate cut by 62 per cent.

Activities

1. Explain **two** of the benefits that flow production seems to have for this business.

2. What are the possible advantages and disadvantages of keeping stocks to an absolute minimum?

The main advantages of flow production

- Low cost of each unit produced due to high levels of output and efficiency. These efficiency gains are the main reason why growing businesses often use flow production.
- High amount of automation with computer-controlled machinery now widely used. This can result in very consistent, high standards of quality.
- Less need to hold stocks. Unlike batch production, production is continuous so it is not necessary to hold high stocks of completed items for a long time.

The main limitations of flow production

- Set-up costs of buying the equipment are high, especially if computer-controlled robots are to be used.

- Production problems can be costly as the whole production line may have to be stopped.

- Worker motivation can be low because they are not involved in making a complete product and doing one repetitive task can become boring.

- The basic standardised product cannot be changed without costly and time-consuming changes in machinery.

Lean production

Businesses increasingly face being trapped between rising costs and increased competition, which forces them to keep prices as low as possible. One approach to tackling this problem is to become more efficient in production. For many firms this means using **lean production** methods.

The Japanese car manufacturer Toyota was the first company in the world to fully adopt this production approach. It is no coincidence that it is now the world's largest and most successful car manufacturer.

Lean production involves using less of all resources – space, materials, stock, time and labour. Some of the main lean production techniques are outlined below.

Key terms

Lean production: a production approach that aims to use fewer resources by using them more efficiently.

A *Flow production increases output and efficiency*

Kaizen

Kaizen literally means 'continuous improvement'. In terms of operations management this means involving and encouraging workers to make suggestions for small and frequent improvements. These small improvements (in quality, reducing waste or finding better ways of making a good) will eventually add up to a huge increase in efficiency. Many businesses now have kaizen groups in which workers and supervisors meet regularly to suggest and discuss improvements within the business.

Just-in-time manufacturing

Money tied up in stocks is money wasted, according to the **just-in-time manufacturing (JIT)** principle. If stocks of materials, spare parts and completed products are reduced to zero, or at most an absolute minimum, then the money saved could be used in other parts of the business. This can be achieved by:

- arranging with suppliers that all supply orders are only brought to the business on the day required, not days or weeks in advance
- producing to order, not for stock – this means only making products when they have been ordered by a customer not just to add to stocks of unsold goods.

Case study

The costs of holding large stocks of flour, sugar, salt, oil and other baking ingredients were reducing the profits of BakeitWell Bakery. The small family firm had a lot of competition from local supermarkets. The owners prided themselves on producing quality bread, rolls and cakes of all shapes and sizes to meet customers' tastes. Ahmed, the son of the founder, had just completed his GCSE Business Studies course and he suggested to the other members of the family firm that: 'We should order all of our supplies just as we need them. I could work out a simple computer programme that would tell us when to re-order supplies for the next two or three days. At the moment we have about three weeks supplies in stock.'

The others agreed and the new JIT plan went well for three months. Stock holding costs fell. Then a fire at the main flour suppliers stopped deliveries for two weeks. Many of BakeitWell's customers were disappointed that they could not buy their regular orders.

Activities

1. Explain what just-in-time stock ordering means.

2. Do you think it was a good idea for BakeitWell Bakery to introduce this system of stock ordering? Explain your answer.

B *Advantages and disadvantages of JIT manufacturing*

Advantages	Disadvantages
Cuts stock-holding costs and increases efficient use of factory space.	Customers have to wait for goods to be made as completed goods are not held in stock. Some customers may prefer to buy from stock.
Capital that was used to pay for stocks can now be used more efficiently in other parts of the business.	Costs of ordering supplies could increase as so many small orders are made rather than one order and one large delivery of supplies.
Improves efficiency of cash flow by reducing the time between paying for supplies and receiving payment from customers.	Requires very reliable suppliers and transport systems – any hold-ups or problems with either of these could lead to output being stopped as supplies have not arrived.
Close contact with suppliers at all times leads to better, more efficient supplier relationships (e.g. willingness to supply goods at very short notice).	

Lean design

There are great advantages in launching a new product or invention before competitors. Just think of the benefits gained by Apple from its launch of the iPhone in 2008, months before its competitors' products. Some of the features of **lean design** include:

- Saving time in developing and launching new products means that firms can charge high prices and make substantial profits, before lowering prices as competitors come into the market.
- Lean design involves teams of designers working on different parts of a product simultaneously, before bringing all parts together in the final product.
- This time-saving approach is much easier than it used to be, thanks to computer-aided design (CAD) programs that can link up one design team with others. CAD also allows the computer to do a lot of work that would previously have been undertaken by building models and prototypes.

C   *Computer-aided design allows businesses to get new products into the market quicker – another form of lean production*

Cell production

This is a variation on pure flow production. Instead of each individual worker just doing one repetitive task, the total job is split into complete units of work that can be done by teams or 'cells' of workers. So, for example, a team of workers can assemble a complete washing machine rather than each worker just adding one part to it as it passes by on a production line.

This approach requires flexible and well-trained staff because they must be able to do more than one small task during production and they need training in problem-solving and decision-making. For these reasons, cell production (and this includes most forms of team-working) is said to be much more motivating and rewarding for workers than traditional flow production, with its emphasis on doing one repetitive task with no chance of individual decision-making.

Many business owners set growth as one of the objectives for their firm. The directors controlling even the largest of public limited companies usually have business expansion as one of their main aims. For example, the President of Coca-Cola once suggested that his aim was for more of this soft drink to be consumed around the world than water!

Toyota cell production makes it even leaner

The Toyota Production System (TPS) is the world-famous lean production method that tries to achieve three important aims:

- Provide customers with quality, reliable vehicles at the lowest cost.
- Provide workers with job satisfaction.
- Give flexibility to respond to market changes.

Cell production is an important part of this. Teams of workers are given complete units to make, such as the front suspension. Team leaders are expected to work too and to encourage suggestions from team members. The team has decision-making power over some issues, such as who does what job and when to maintain and repair machinery. Toyota makes some of the most reliable cars in the world.

Activities

1 Explain why cell production might:
a lead to higher quality output
b lead to more motivated staff than traditional flow production.

2 Why is it important for businesses to be flexible to be able to respond to market changes?

3 How might lean production make it easier for a business to respond to market changes?

Case study

■ Benefits of business growth

Marketing and financial advantages include:

- Greater market share, which is important to retailers (they will be keener to stock the product) and consumers (who may want to buy the most popular products).
- Increased revenue should lead to greater profit if costs do not rise at an even faster rate.

Operations management advantages include:

- Reductions in unit cost. This advantage can make a business more competitive.

Large businesses usually have unit cost advantages over smaller businesses in the same industry. This does not meant that the total costs of running Tesco are less than the cost of operating Waitrose. Tesco's annual sales are many times greater than those of Waitrose, but its total costs are too. However, the cost of Tesco's operations per unit sold are much lower. There are several possible reasons for this. Collectively they are called **economies of scale**.

Main economies of scale

Bulk-buying or purchasing economies

Tesco is able to order thousands of boxes of breakfast cereal at a time, so the manufacturer will offer lower average prices than to a supermarket ordering just hundreds of boxes. Delivering one very large order will be cheaper than delivering many smaller orders.

Technical economies

Larger factories and pieces of equipment are more efficient than smaller ones. A large mechanical digger still only needs one driver, as does a small digger, yet the earth and rock it can move will be much greater. A large business is likely to be able to buy the latest and most productive computer-controlled machines. These would be too expensive for small firms. In addition, the larger business can keep these machines used most of the time, which further reduces average costs.

Specialist managers

As a firm expands it can afford to employ specialist managers who should improve efficiency, compared to a small business where the owner has to perform accounting, production, human resources and other management roles.

Financial economies

Large firms have cost advantages when they raise finance. Large firms borrowing very large sums of money that offer high security to the bank will obtain lower interest rates than a riskier loan to a smaller business.

Possible disadvantages of growth

Business expansion has its limits too, otherwise all goods and services would be produced by one massive organisation with maximum economies of scale. There are problems that most large businesses face, which can lead to increases in average costs. These are called diseconomies of scale.

Main diseconomies of scale

Poor communication

Sending and receiving messages becomes less effective:

- The organisational structure has more levels. Messages from the top to the bottom of the organisation take longer and pass through more managers' hands. Messages can become distorted or even arrive too late.
- IT becomes more widely used. IT communication and e-mails are much more widely used in large rather than small businesses. This is often because it becomes much more difficult to meet people and to explain and discuss issues face-to-face. E-mails have led to a huge growth in the number of messages sent and received, yet only a small proportion of them are important.

Poor motivation

Although large organisations offer more chance of promotion and variety, many workers feel uninvolved. Managers may be far away and difficult to contact. Each worker may feel quite unimportant. This can lead to low motivation and low productivity.

Poor coordination

Most large businesses have operations in many locations and countries:

- It becomes difficult to make sure that all major decisions fit in with the aims of the head office. Conflicting decisions could lead to wastage and higher costs or duplication of resources, for example, similar research being done in more than one of the company's bases.
- Complex production processes with parts and components being made in so many different locations. Any small hold-up or transport problem could cause a loss of output in other plants owned by the business. This would raise average costs.

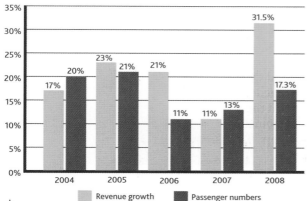

A *Graph showing passenger/revenue growth for EasyJet*

A **quality product** is one that meets the expectations of the customer. It does not necessarily mean 'the best product possible'. The 'best light bulb' could be made to last for 20 years, but would customers be prepared to pay £10 for it? Customers' expectation of a £1 light bulb is that it should not fail for about two years after purchase – this is enough 'quality' to meet expectations. There is no point in spending money on making one last for 20 years.

Large businesses often have quality problems, which means that the product or service can fail to meet customers' expectations for it.

Main causes of quality problems

Poorly motivated workers

If workers in an expanding business are not well-managed or well-motivated then they may not be keen to produce a good product or provide a quality customer service. The reputation of the business will then be damaged. This could increase the cost of replacing faulty goods or repeating customer service up to a higher standard.

No clear responsibility for quality

Whose job is it to make sure high-quality levels are met? The quality inspector? The managers? The workers? If there is no clear guidance about this then goods and services may fail the quality test.

Lack of consistency

A shop with many branches may fail to give consistent quality customer service. One branch might change or exchange unwanted goods with no time limit – another branch might limit this to two weeks' purchase.

Outsourcing

Using other firms to make parts of a product or to provide customer service can lead to low quality. These **outsourcing** firms may not work to the same standards so strict quality checks may be necessary, which could increase inspection costs.

Inspection costs

Unless every worker is made accountable for quality (see Total Quality Management opposite), then inspectors or checkers will be needed to check regularly that **quality standards** are being met. In retail these might be 'mystery shoppers' who report back on levels of customer service, while in factories they will be quality-control inspectors. This is called **quality assurance**.

Objectives

Understand how to identify quality problems and the causes of them.

Understand the methods businesses can use to maintain consistent quality.

Key terms

Quality product: goods or service that meets customers' expectations and is therefore 'fit for purpose'.

Outsourcing: using the businesses to make all or part of a product or provide an aspect of the customer care.

Quality standards: the expectations of customers expressed in terms of the minimum acceptable production or service standards.

Quality assurance: setting and trying to meet quality standards throughout the business.

Total Quality Management (TQM): an approach to quality that aims to involve all employees in the quality improvement process.

Main methods of maintaining quality

Setting agreed quality standards

Once customer expectations are known for a product (perhaps by asking them through market research), minimum quality standards have to be set at each stage of the business.

Examples include:

- **Banks** – maximum waiting time to see a cashier or to have a telephone call answered. Quality assurance would involve keeping a check on whether this minimum time was being kept to.
- **Fast food delivery** – maximum time for deliveries to be made. Quality assurance would involve recording delivery times to see if these were within the maximum level set.
- **Jet engines** – maximum failure rate of each component (e.g. once in every 100,000 hours of operation). Quality assurance would not involve testing each component produced to destruction. However, strict quality standards would be set for each stage of the production process.
- **Batteries** – minimum number of hours of continuous operation. Quality assurance would test a certain number of batteries after a set number had been produced.

Sometimes these quality standards are printed in company literature or in shops so that customers are aware of what they can expect from the product and the service the company provides.

A *A Rolls-Royce aircraft engine. Customer expectations of reliability mean that these are constructed to the highest possible quality standards*

Total Quality Management (TQM)

The **Total Quality Management (TQM)** approach to quality requires the involvement of all employees in an organisation. It is based on the principle that everyone within a business can contribute to the overall quality of the finished product or service.

TQM often involves a significant change in the way an organisation works. Employees can no longer think that quality is someone else's responsibility. Instead, the search for quality is everyone's responsibility. When adopting this concept, every worker should think about the quality of the work they are performing because another employee is, in effect, their internal customer. Consider these examples:

- A truck driver who drops off supplies to retailers is the internal customer of the team loading the vehicle – goods must be handled carefully and loaded in the right order. The truck driver has to face the retailer if goods are damaged or the wrong ones delivered.
- A computer assembly team is the internal customer of the teams producing the individual components – a fault with any of these means the assembled computer will not meet quality standards.

The TQM concept has revolutionised the way all workers are asked to consider quality. To be effective the concept must be fully explained and training given to all staff in its scope and the techniques used to put it into effect.

Case study

Hydrapower Dynamics Ltd makes hydraulic hoses – tubes that carry compressed air. The market is very competitive. The company has contracts to supply aircraft parts makers who insist on 100 per cent delivery, on time and no faults in parts over a 12-month period. The company's 60 workers are involved in all aspects of quality. They take part in problem-solving teams to put TQM into practice. In effect, each worker is a quality inspector too.

Activities

1   Why is quality important to Hydrapower Dynamics Ltd?

2   Do you think TQM is the best way to achieve high quality? Explain your answer.

11.1 Stages of Controlled Assessment

So what are the stages involved in carrying out Controlled Assessment? Essentially, there are three stages, each of which has a specific level of control: high, medium or low.

For GCSE Business Studies each stage is as follows:

- Task setting
- Task taking
- Task marking

In this section we shall look at the first two stages.

Objectives

Understand the stages of Controlled Assessment.

Gain ideas on how to go about researching the task.

Gain tips on how to present your work.

Task setting

Tasks will generally be published every January by the Examination Board for both units and will be available for one assessment opportunity only. Each year there will be a new task set. This means that you will be able to complete the Controlled Assessment after one year of study.

The set task will always be based on the key areas of Unit 1 (also known as Unit 13 for the students taking the Short Course), which is found at the beginning of this book. This means that as you study the Unit, you will be able to develop a greater understanding and knowledge of the issues, and be in a strong position to demonstrate how well and how proficient you have become in developing the skills being assessed. As with coursework, Controlled Assessment will give you the opportunity to investigate an area of business in considerable depth. These areas may be:

- starting a business
- marketing
- finance
- people in business
- operations management.

Task taking

Task taking is completed under limited supervision, meaning that you can carry out your research outside of school lessons at home.

There are different parts to task taking and these are preparation, research and planning.

Preparation

Your investigation will be based on the content that you have already studied from Unit 1 (or Unit 13). Your teacher will have already taught you the relevant information and topics – there will be nothing new to learn but you should remind yourself and make sure you are familiar with what you have already learnt from this unit.

Research and planning

Research and planning will be a very important part of the Controlled Assessment, as they allow you to demonstrate your ability to work independently and extract relevant information from a range of source materials. Research and planning will also allow you to take ownership of your work, and it is for this reason that your research and data collection are undertaken with limited supervisory control.

Working in groups is allowed, but you must remember that your final presentation should be entirely your own work and is not the work of anyone else in your group. You are expected to produce an individually written response to the task that you are set and you will be monitored and supervised by a teacher at all stages of the process. Access to books, the internet and other sources of information will also be controlled.

It will be important to plan ahead what research methods are most likely to be suitable to the task. Making a list of all the different sorts of research tasks you can undertake would be a good starting point.

You will be allowed to complete your research, both in and out of school, and the focus here should be on both primary and secondary methods.

What sort of research should I use?

There are many different methods of research which can be used and these are outlined below.

Desk research

Desk research will involve you collecting information and data which has already been published and is readily available. This type of research is also called secondary research because the information that you will collect is not first-hand information. This information is usually obtained from:

- books
- public libraries
- company reports
- government statistics
- research organisations
- the internet
- newspaper reports.

Your local Chamber of Commerce and other local trade associations are good sources of information. Desk research has several advantages in that it is readily available and can be easily accessed. It does have its disadvantages – information is often out-of-date and may not necessarily be what you require.

AQA **Examiner's tip**

Re-read your notes from what you have studied in Unit 1 (Unit 13) and make sure that you are really familiar with the topics.

AQA **Examiner's tip**

It is important that you use both primary and secondary sources of research. Both types of research carry equal weight and your teacher and the moderator will be looking for evidence of them in your Controlled Assessment task.

links

See Chapter 2 for more information on primary and secondary market research methods.

Key terms

Desk research: information which is gathered from secondary sources.

During these sessions you will be allowed access to your research folder and all work will be collected in at the end of the session. You will not be allowed to take your presentation home with you.

You are not expected to rewrite all the findings of your research, but you should attach key pieces of information as appendices.

AQA Examiner's tip

Think carefully before the writing-up sessions start on how you are going to present the information that you have researched.

Tips on presenting your work

Make sure that you address each of the bullet points specified on the Controlled Assessment task sheet.

The task you will be set will always state clearly what you are expected to do. →	You are a consultant working for marketing company. You have been approached by a local business person and asked to prepare a report recommending how to improve performance for an existing small business which is experiencing a decline in sales. The business specialises in one main type of product or service.
The information/data that you have collected should address the task and sources of information, as well as your reasons for their choice, should be clearly stated. →	**Research and planning** In your report you need to: • conduct research to identify an appropriate business that meets the above criteria • identify the current target market for the product or service • explain and analyse appropriate ways to improve the performance of the business • make some firm recommendations which illustrate clearly that you have identified the best strategies possible.
It is not enough to simply present information you will need to fully explain and analyse all the information you are intending to use, giving clear reasons for your choice. →	**Final presentation** Your presentation must be produced under controlled conditions. You will have up to three hours to complete this work. This can be split over a number of sessions supervised by your teacher.
In addressing each of the bullet-pointed outcomes, you need to show clearly that you have used both primary and secondary sources of information. →	Your presentation should contain: • the target market of the business • the results of your market research • your recommendations on how the business can improve performance • a conclusion explaining why your strategies will be particularly effective.

C Example of what a task may look like

Your results should be presented in a number of ways, using a range of presentation techniques such as bar charts, graphs, relevant interview selections and observations. This is a very important point, so do think carefully beforehand about how you will present your information.

It is important to use business terms and ideas throughout your work. The terms used must be applied to the task and not just be a descriptive account that could have been copied from a textbook. Link your use of business terms and concepts to the question under consideration, making sure that you use them to answer the question.

Before you start the writing-up session you should have thought about the information you are going to use in your final presentation. Say why you have made particular selections and how they help to address the issue. You need to analyse and interpret your information, explaining what it shows and how it relates to the problem which has been set.

Finally, it is important that you make judgements and draw conclusions throughout your work, in order to support your overall conclusion. You will be expected to make a final judgement regarding the issue.

Breakdown of favourite flavour of milkshakes and size

D Your results should be presented in a variety of ways such as bar graphs

11.2 How your Controlled Assessment will be marked

The third and final stage of Controlled Assessment is the marking of your work. Your work will be marked and assessed by your teacher according to AQA's assessment criteria. Some samples from your school will then be sent to a moderator who works for AQA and they will compare this work with other schools.

It is essential that you address all the key elements of the Controlled Assessment task, as your teacher and the moderator will be looking for evidence of your understanding of the business world.

In order to gain high marks for the Controlled Assessment, you need to show evidence that the work has been well researched, with the research being directed to the specified business problem. Work of a descriptive nature will not generate high marks. You should write in a succinct, discursive style, making sure that any information that you use is fully explained and analysed. You will be required to display your conceptual, analytical and evaluative skills throughout your work. In order to do this, it is important that you have an understanding of how your work will be assessed and marked.

The marking criteria for Controlled Assessment

There are three assessment objectives against which your work will be marked.

AO1 Recall, select and communicate knowledge and understanding of concepts, issues and terminology.

AO2 Apply skills, knowledge and understanding in a variety of contexts and in planning and carrying out investigations and tasks.

AO3 Analyse and evaluate evidence, make reasoned judgements and present appropriate conclusions.

The Controlled Assessment is worth a total of 40 marks towards your overall grade.

Assessment Objective 1

Recall, select and communicate their knowledge and understanding of concepts, issues and terminology.

As you conduct your research to resolve the business issue you are looking at, there should be evidence that your research has been gathered from a variety of sources, as mentioned earlier.

Have I collected information from:	yes/no	notes
The internet		
Surveys/questionaires		
Observations		
Visits		
Interviews		
Textbooks		

Read **Item C** and then answer the questions that follow.

Item C

Freddie is a sole trader. He rents a small workshop in the centre of town.

He makes gold jewellery to his own designs using job production. He sells each item for an average of £50. In a typical month he makes and sells 30 items. Each piece of jewellery costs Freddie £6 to make. He pays £50 per month to advertise in a local newspaper.

Another jewellery maker has set up in business in the same town as Freddie. This offers a more limited range of designs and uses cheaper gold than Freddie does. However, this new business sells items at lower prices than Freddie.

---

3   (a) Using **Item C**, calculate how much profit Freddie makes each month. Show all of your workings out clearly. *(5 marks)*

    (b) i)   Explain ONE advantage to Freddie's business of using job production. *(2 marks)*

        ii) Explain ONE disadvantage to Freddie's business of using job production. *(2 marks)*

    (c) Explain TWO factors that Freddie should have considered when choosing the location for his business. *(6 marks)*

    (d) Discuss how Freddie might respond to the competition from the new jewellery business. Give reasons for your answer. *(9 marks)*

■ UNIT 2 Examination-style questions

Read **Item A** and then answer the questions that follow.

Item A

Headstart Ltd is a small chain of hairdressers. It offers cutting and hair colouring for both women and men. The directors plan to expand the business by opening further salons. This will mean recruiting and selecting several new staff who will be offered 'off-the-job' training before working full time for Headstart.

Staff in existing salons are paid wages but can earn bonuses for receiving good customer reports on the feedback form that is given out to all customers. The directors are very keen to keep all of the existing staff and they are looking at others ways of motivating them.

---

1   (a) What is meant by 'off-the-job' training? *(2 marks)*

    (b) Explain briefly, two reasons why it is important for Headstart Ltd to train all new employees. *(5 marks)*

    (c) i)   Apart from increasing wages, identify TWO possible methods for motivating staff at Headstart Ltd. *(2 marks)*

        ii) Explain which of these methods you would recommend Headstart Ltd to use. Give reasons for your answer. *(5 marks)*

Read **Item B** and then answer the questions that follow.

Item B

In the town where the largest Headstart salon is located, competition has recently increased with the opening of a branch of a large national chain of hairdressers. It has a wide product portfolio.

It offers a range of beauty treatments in addition to hairdressing. It is offering prices 20% less than the Headstart salon – but this may just be for a short period of time.

The directors of Headstart are planning changes to the company's marketing mix to respond to increased competition. These changes will have to be successful if the company is to have any chance of expanding. The company only advertises on local radio stations at present and offers no promotions to customers.

---

2   (a) Explain TWO benefits to Headstart Ltd of increasing its product portfolio.   *(5 marks)*

     (b) Explain TWO ways in which Headstart Ltd could use promotion to attract more customers.   *(5 marks)*

     (c) Recommend which pricing methods Headstart Ltd could use to help it expand its business. Give reasons for your answer.   *(9 marks)*

Read **Item C** and then answer the questions that follow.

Item C

At a board meeting, the directors of Headstart Ltd discussed two alternative locations for the next new salon. Site A is in a busy town centre. A suitable shop is available but the rent is high. There are several other salons in the town. Site B is on a small housing estate with no competitors. The rent would be lower but parking is very limited.

Headstart Ltd has a great reputation for customer service. The directors want the quality of service to be high in the new location too.

---

3   (a) Explain ONE reason why good quality customer service is important to Headstart Ltd.   *(2 marks)*

     (b) Explain ONE way in which this hairdressing business could offer good customer service.   *(4 marks)*

     (c) Recommend to the directors of Headstart Ltd the most suitable location for the new salon. Give reasons for your answer.   *(9 marks)*

Direct mail: sending promotional material directly to consumers.

Direct marketing: using direct means to contact consumers to increase sales (e.g. e-mail, telemarketing and direct mail).

Diseconomies of scale: the production costs of each item rises as a firm expands.

Diversification: joining two businesses in different industries (e.g. an insurance company merges with a publishing business).

Diversify: spreading risk by selling in different markets.

Dividend: payment made to shareholders from company profits – usually made annually.

Division of labour: breaking a job down into small, repetitive tasks that can be done quickly by workers specialised in this one task.

Divorce between ownership and control: when directors control a public limited company and thousands of shareholders own it, but the two groups may have different objectives.

E

e-commerce: transactions between people and business carried out entirely via the internet.

Economies of scale: the average costs of each item fall as a firm expands.

Employee: anyone who works for a business or organisation.

Employer: a business or organisation that employs a worker.

Enterprise: the ability to handle uncertainty and recognise change.

Entrepreneur: an individual with an idea for a business.

Environmental objective: a business aim to protect the environment during its operations (e.g. to recycle waste water). This will reduce social costs.

Ethical objective: a business aim to 'do the right thing' according to the values and beliefs of managers, even if this is not the most profitable way (e.g. pay workers in low-wage countries above average rates).

Ethics: the moral grounds on which decisions are made and the impact the business has on its internal and external environment.

Extension strategies: steps taken to extend the life cycle of the product.

External recruitment: appointing an employee of another business to fill a vacancy.

F

Flow production: large-scale production where each stage of production is carried out one after the other, continuously, on a production line.

Focus group: in-depth discussion with a small group of consumers (8–10), which probes their feelings towards a product or service.

Forecast: a technique where the business attempts to estimate future sales, cash flow or other financial variables.

Franchise: the legal right to use the name and logo of an existing firm and sell the same products.

Franchisee: the firm that buys the franchise rights from the existing business.

Franchisor: the existing firm that sells the franchise rights to another business.

Fringe benefits: rewards to employees that do not involve the direct payment of money to them.

Full-time workers: working for the normal full working week (e.g. 36 hours).

Funding: the capital (money) provided for the various stages of business growth by different sources of finance, either on a short- or long-term basis.

G

Gap in the market: a business opportunity that is either a completely new idea or adds something different to an existing product or service.

Globalisation: increasing trend for goods to be traded internationally and for companies to locate abroad.

Grants: money given to a business by a government organisation or charity.

Gross profit: the difference between sales revenue and cost of making the products sold.

Gross profit = sales revenue – cost of sales

Gross profit margin: the percentage of sales revenue that is gross profit.

Gross profit margin % = (gross profit ÷ sales revenue) × 100

Growth: an increase in turnover (sales), market share or profit.

H

Horizontal integration: joining two businesses in the same industry and stage of production (e.g. two hairdressing businesses).

I

Incorporation: the process of forming a limited liability company such as a Ltd or plc.

Induction training: initial training to familiarise new recruits with the systems of a business.

Information communication technology (ICT): the use of electronic technology to gather, store, process and communicate information.

Inorganic growth: expansion by merging with or taking over another business.

Internal recruitment: appointing an existing employee of the business to fill a vacancy.

Internet research: using information that has already been published on the internet to gather information about the market for a firm's products or services.

Internet selling: marketing products through the business's website.

Job analysis: identifying the tasks and skills needed to perform a job well.

Job description: a detailed statement of the nature of the job and the tasks involved.

Job production: making one-off, specialised products for each customer.

Just-in-time manufacturing (JIT): ordering supplies so that they arrive just when they are needed and making goods only when ordered by customers.

Kaizen: continuous improvement.

L

Layers of management: the number of different levels of management and responsibility in a structure.

Lean design: producing new designs as quickly as possible.

Lean production: a production approach that aims to use fewer resources by using them more efficiently.

Liabilities: debts owed by a business.

Limited company: a business recognised as a legal unit that offers investors (shareholders) limited liability.

Limited liability: investors (shareholders) in a limited company can only lose their investment in the business if it fails; they cannot be forced to sell assets to pay off the firm's debts.

Liquidity: how easy it is for a business to pay its short-term debts.

Loan from friends and family: finance provided by friends or family where the interest rate and repayment periods are agreed with them.

Logistics: the process of buying, managing and delivering goods, from the point of manufacture to the end consumer.

Loss: when revenue is less than costs.

Loss-leader pricing: setting a price below cost hoping to gain other profitable sales.

M

Mail order: direct marketing through mail shots leading to goods being delivered directly to the customer.

Marketing budget: the amount to be spent on marketing and promotion over a certain period of time.

Marketing mix: the four major variables for which decisions must be made when marketing a product.

Market research: research that enables a firm to find out about its market, its customers and its potential customers.

Market share: the proportion of total market sales sold by one business.

Merger: an agreement between business owners to combine two businesses and operate as a larger one.

Monopoly: any business with more than a 25 per cent market share.

Mortgage: long-term loan for purchasing a building.

Motivated: the will to work due to the enjoyment of the work itself.

Multinational: a business with operations in more than one country.

N

Net cash flow: difference between cash in and cash out of a business over a time period.

Net profit: the difference between sales revenue and total costs of the business.
Net profit = gross profit – overheads

Net profit margin: the percentage of sales revenue that is net profit.
Net profit margin % = (net profit ÷ sales revenue) × 100

Non-monetary rewards: rewards to employees that do not involve the direct payment of money to them. Also called 'fringe benefits'.

O

Off-shoring: making products or parts of products in other countries. Services can be off-shored too, as with telephone call centres moving to India.

Off-the-job training: takes place away from the job at another place (e.g. the business's training centre or a college).

On-the-job training: takes place when employees receive training as they are working at the place of work.

Opening balance: the money the business has at the start of the month. It is the closing balance from the previous month.

Operational efficiency: producing goods and services to an acceptable standard with as few resources as possible to keep costs per unit low.

Organic growth: expansion from within the business (e.g. by opening more shop branches).

Organisational structure: the internal links between managers and workers showing lines of authority.

Overdraft: a flexible arrangement that allows a business to spend more money than it has in its bank account, as and when it needs the finance.

Overheads: expenses of the business that are not directly part of the production process (e.g. rent and management salaries).

P

Partnership: the simplest way two or more people can be in business together, where partners are jointly and personally responsible for debts.

Part-time workers: working for a proportion of the full working week (e.g. 18 hours).

Penetration pricing: setting a price at a low level to gain greater market share.

Pension: payments made to retired workers. In addition to the state pension, businesses are expected to offer their own pension schemes.

Person specification: a profile of the type of person likely to make a good applicant.

Personal selling: employing a person to visit potential customers to persuade them to buy your goods or services.

Place: the methods used by a firm to sell its products or services to consumers.

Pop-up: an internet advert that 'pops up' in a new window when visiting another company's website.

Price: the amount charged by a business for its product or service.

Price skimming: setting a price at a high level to create a high-quality and exclusive image.

Primary research: gathering new information specifically for the purposes identified by the business.

Private limited company (Ltd): a company that cannot sell shares to the general public. It is not listed on the Stock Exchange.

Product: the service or physical good being sold by the company.

Product differentiation: attempting to make your products stand out from those of your rivals through advertising, design or different product features.

Product life cycle: the lifespan of a product, recorded in sales from launch to being taken off the market.

Product portfolio/product mix: the range of products sold by a business.

Product range: the collective term given to all the products made or sold by a business.

Profit: what is left after costs have been deducted from revenue.

Profit = revenue – costs

Profit and loss account: this shows whether the business made a profit or loss over the last period (usually a year). It is also known as the income statement.

Profit margin: profit made as a proportion of sales revenue.

Promotion: all the ways a business communicates to consumers with the aim of selling products.

Promotional mix: the combination of promotion methods used by a business.

Public limited company (plc): a company able to sell shares to the general public by being listed on the Stock Exchange.

Publicity: gaining press coverage for your business.

Q

Quality assurance: a system of agreeing and meeting quality standards at each stage of production.

Quality product: goods or service that meet customers' expectations and is therefore 'fit for purpose'.

Quality standards: the expectations of customers expressed in terms of the minimum acceptable production or service standards.

Questionnaire: a set of questions designed to discover information relating to a product or service.

R

Recruitment: attracting people to apply for a job vacancy.

Retained profit: profit kept in the business after tax and dividends have been paid.

Revenue: the amount of money a business receives from selling goods or services.

Risk: the potential for loss but rewards in business make it a calculated gamble.

Robot: a computer-controlled machine able to perform a physical task.

S

Salary: when a worker is paid a fixed amount per month or year, no matter what hours they work.

Sale and leaseback: selling an asset, such as a building, to a leasing company and paying an annual leasing charge so that the asset can still be used.

Sales: the amount sold or the value sold (e.g. 200 units or £400).

Sales promotion: activities to attract consumer attention to a product to increase sales.

Sales revenue: the value of goods sold.

Sales revenue = number of goods sold × price

Secondary research: research that uses information that has already been gathered for another purpose.

Shareholders: part owners of a limited company – they own shares in it.

Shares issued: value of shares bought by shareholders.

Social benefits: the benefits of a business activity, not just to the firm but to society (e.g. new jobs created by business expansion).

Social costs: the costs of business activity, including both financial costs paid by the firm and the costs on society (e.g. factory pollution).

Social enterprise: an activity that achieves a reward for society.

Sole trader: the most common and most simple form of business organisation, often just one person.

Span of control: the number of junior employees each manager is directly responsible for.

Specialisation: work is divided into separate tasks or jobs that allow workers to become skilled at one of them.

Sponsorship: a business pays for an activity or an event to gain publicity.

Stakeholder: an individual or group with an interest in a business, such as employees, customers, managers, shareholders, suppliers, competitors and the local community.

Supplier feedback: gathering information from companies that supply products or services on their forecasts for what is likely to happen in the market in the future.

T

Takeover: purchasing another business from its owners.

Target market: the group of consumers aimed at by the business.

Technology: in relation to business location, this refers to the use of e-technology, such as the internet and e-mail, to create a virtual market between the business and the consumer.

Telephone survey: a series of set questions delivered over the telephone to consumers as a method of primary research.

Telesales: selling to the customer through telephone contact alone.

Total Quality Management (TQM): an approach to quality that aims to involve all employees in the quality improvement process.

Trade credit: suppliers who allow debts for goods and services to be paid one or two months after delivery.

Turnover: the value of sales made during a trading period, also called revenue.

U

Uncertainty: not knowing the future, or what is going to happen.

Unit cost: the average cost of making each unit.

Unit cost = total cost ÷ output

Unlimited liability: unincorporated businesses, such as sole traders and partnerships, have unlimited liability, which means that the owners are responsible for all the business's debts.

V

Vertical backward integration: joining two businesses in the same industry but a different stage of production, towards the supplier (e.g. a computer manufacturer's takeover of a 'chip' maker).

Vertical forward integration: joining two businesses in the same industry but a different stage of production, towards the customer (e.g. a farmer's takeover of a butcher's shop).

W

Wage: when an employee is paid a fixed amount for each hour or day they work.

Website: many businesses now have their own website on the internet to provide information about their business for consumers.

Wholesaler: middleman or distributor that buys in bulk, holds stocks and sells mainly to retailers not consumers.

Word-of-mouth recommendation: getting customers to talk to their friends and family about your product or service.

Index

Acknowledgements

The authors and pulisher are grateful to the following for permission to reproduce the following copyright material:

Text acknowledgements: ASOS case study adapted from *The Guardian* www.guardian.co.uk; Directa Ltd extract www.directa.co.uk, reprinted with permission; ChipsAway item – see www.chipsaway.co.uk; Lloyds TSB case study adapted from BBC article www.bbc.co.uk; Rolls-Royce case study adapted from Times Online http://business.timesonline.co.uk; Electrolux case study adapted from www.bbc.co.uk/1/hi/england/wear/7143839; Federation of European Employers table adapted from their website www.fedee.com/; Burberry extract from *The Guardian* http://www.guardian.co.uk/business/2007/feb/28/politics.economicpolicy; ASOS case study adapted from www.asos.com; E.on statement adapted from www.timesonline.co.uk; Brand Republic extract see www.brandrepublic.com; Advertising during X-Factor adapted from www.telegraph.co.uk/finance; Coke Zero item www.usatoday.com/finance; Competitors promotions extract adapted from www.bnet.com/retail; Marks & Spencers and Taxi Promotions UK reproduced by kind permission of Taxi Promotions www.taxipromotions.com; ASOS website see www.asos.com; Sainsbury case study adapted from Times Online www.timesonline.co.uk; British Petroleum case study adapted from http://spectator.advfn.com/; HSBC case study adapted from http://hsbc.com; Santander case study adapted from BBC article www.bbc.co1/hi/business7719859; Yell's debt mountain case study adapted from http://business.timesonline.co.uk; MacDonald's workers' pay dispute case study adapted from www.nzherald.co.nz; Activity on BP adapted from http://newsvote.bbc.co.uk; Gorton's manufacturing system case study adapted from www.advancedmanufacturing.com/index.php/Lean-Manufacturing-Case-Study.html; Acme International case study adapted from www.acme-international.com/; Toyota case study see www.toyota.co.jp/en/vision/production_system/; Hydrapower Dynamics Ltd case study www.dti.gov.uk/quality/casestudies © Crown Copyright reprinted under Crown Copyright PSI License C2008002303; Picking a business case study *Sunday Times* 19 October 2003 *http://business.timesonline.co.uk/tol/business/article995843.ece* reprinted with permission from News International (NI); Eskimimi screengrab – see www.eskimimi.com/; The Poverty Site, www.poverty.org.uk, reprinted with permission.

Photograph acknowledgements: Chapter 1 opener: Alamy/Tetra Images; 1.2A, Gü; 1.2C, Alamy/Hugh Threlfall; 1.3B, Alamy/Photofusion Picture Library; 1.3C, Fotolia; 1.4B, Fotolia; 1.5A, PA Photos/AP; 1.6A, 4 x iStockphoto; 1.7A Fotolia; 1.8A, Fotolia; 1.8B, iStockphoto; 1.9A, iStockphoto; 1.9C, courtesy of Deli 28; 1.10B, Alamy/stock-wales; 1.11B, iStockphoto; 1.11C, PA Photos/AP; Chapter 2 opener, 2.1B, Alamy/Martin Bond; 2.1C, courtesy of *The Grocer*; 2.2A, iStockphoto; 2.3A, Alamy/Drive Images; 2.4A, *left* Alamy/Mint Photography, *right* Alamy/JLImages; 2.5A, Alamy/Caro; 2.5B, iStockphoto; 2.6A, Alamy/Jim Wileman; 2.7B, 5.7B, courtesy of www.eskimimi.com; 2.7C, Nelson Thornes/Kerboodle; Chapter 3 opener, iStockphoto; 3.1B, Alamy/ICP; 3.2B, Alamy/Ladi Kim; 3.4B, Alamy/Keith Morris; Chapter 4 opener, 4.1E, Alamy/Jupiter Images/Creatas; 4.1B, 4.1C, 4.1D iStockphoto; 4.1G, Alamy/LondonPhotos – Homer Sykes; 4.3A, 4.3B, 4.4C, iStockphoto; Chapter 5 opener, 5.3A, Getty Images/AFP; 5.1A (centre), Alamy/moodboard; 5.1A (left/right), 5.1D iStockphoto; 5.2A, 5.2C, iStockphoto; 5.3B, Alamy/Justin Kase; 5.4A, Alamy/Alan Gallery; 5.4B, 5.6A, iStockphoto; Chapter 6 opener: Alamy/Keith Morris; 6.1A: Alamy/UK Alan King; 6.2A (top): Alamy/Simon Hadley, (bottom) Alamy/Mark Richardson; 6.2E: Getty Images/AFP/Kazuhiro Nagi; 6.3B: Alamy/NRT – Helena; 6.4C: Rex/Dennis Stone; 6.4D: Alamy/Archimage; 6.5B: /Alamy/Andrew Fox; 6.6A: PA Photos; 6.7A: iStockphoto; 6.7B: Fotolia; 6.7Rolls-Royce: Alamy/Neil McAllister; 6.8B: Still Pictures/sinopictures/Dinodia; 6.8C: Alamy/Alex Segre; Chapter 7 opener: Rex/Sipa Press; 7.1B: Alamy/Helene Rogers; 7.2B: PA Photos/AP; 7.3A: Advertising Archive; 7.4A: iStockphoto; 7.4B: Kerboodle/Nelson Thornes; Chapter 8 opener: iStockphoto; 8.1A: Getty Images/Jason Hawkes; 8.2B: Alamy/Justin Kase Zelevenz; Chapter 9 opener, 9.2C: iStockphoto; 9.3A: Photolibrary/Plus Pix; Chapter 10 opener, 10.1A: Rex/Action Press; 10.1C: Science Photo Library/Brian Bell; 10.3A: Getty Images/Tim Graham; Chapter 11 opener: Alamy/Photofusion Picture Library.